Creative
WIRE JEWELRY

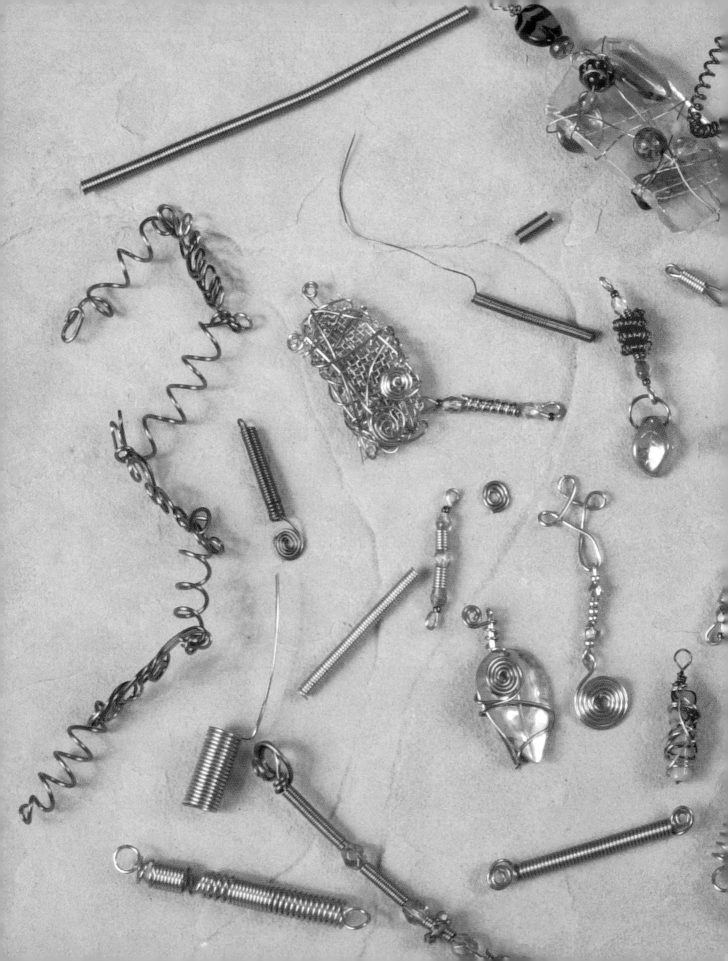

Creative
WIRE JEWELRY

KATHY PETERSON

Photography by Andy Newitt

WATSON-GUPTILL PUBLICATIONS/NEW YORK

Senior Editor: Joy Aquilino
Edited by Anne McNamara
Designed by Areta Buk
Graphic production by Hector Campbell
Text set in 10/14 Berkeley Book

First published in 2001 by Watson-Guptill Publications,
a division of VNU Business Media, Inc.,
770 Broadway, New York, N.Y. 10003
www.watsonguptill.com

Library of Congress Cataloging-in-Publication Data

Kathy Peterson, 1956–
    Creative wire jewelry / Kathy Peterson ; photography by Andy Newitt.
        p.   cm.
    Includes index.
    ISBN 0-8230-1044-9
        1. Jewelry making.   2. Wire craft.   I. Title.

TT212.P49 2001
745.594'2—dc21
                                                    2001026933

Manufactured in Malaysia

First printing, 2001

4 5 6 7 8 9 / 09 08 07 06 05 04 03 02

ACKNOWLEDGMENTS

When I stop and think about it, much of my life has been dedicated to being creative. Even the littlest things have been known to inspire a new design or project. Being around other creative people especially inspires me. In fact, had it not been for a handful of such people, this book would not have been possible. It is with deep gratitude that I would like to thank the following:

First and foremost, I must thank Jack O'Brien, President of Artistic Wire, Ltd., for his vision and dedication to designers like me. His foresight in manufacturing so many beautiful colors and gauges of wire enabled me to create all of the designs featured in this book. He is truly a terrific friend and supportive business associate.

Then there is my dear friend Julianna Hudgins. Without her continued support and encouragement, this book would have been only a dream.

I cannot forget to thank my husband, Tom Knapp, for his support, understanding, and patience during my creative moods and milestones. Thanks, sweetheart.

This book would also not have been possible if it weren't for the creative guidance of my dad and mom, John and Lorraine Peterson. It is from their skills and inspiration that my own talents emerged.

And finally, thanks to Joy Aquilino, my editor. Her guidance, suggestions, and continued assistance have been truly appreciated.

Contents

Preface

As a self-taught jewelry designer, I began working with wire only one-and-a-half years prior to writing this book. I find making wire jewelry fulfilling and an exciting creative outlet. The wire techniques and designs I share with you are easy enough for a beginner to master, yet challenging enough to interest the intermediate crafter. Each design utilizes at least one technique, such as wire wrapping, twisting, beading, coiling, and linking, and often combines several to shape and give character to the pieces.

The incredible range of wires available gives home crafters the opportunity for unlimited creative expression. Feel free to experiment with different wire colors and gauges to develop your own one-of-a-kind pieces. Though you may be tempted to start your wire crafting with traditional silver- or gold-filled wire, you'll find that throughout this book I have used a combination of copper-enamel and silver-enamel wires. These wires are not only more economical, they have a colorful and contemporary appearance that is well suited to today's spirited fashions.

On the following pages are dozens of stylish and innovative designs that you can re-create or use as inspiration. Each project is clearly presented, with easy-to-follow step-by-step photography to guide you from start to finish. Choose from a variety of unique and original projects for wire necklaces, earrings, bracelets, rings, and hair accessories. The tools and materials you'll need are quite affordable and readily available in craft and hobby shops. Best of all, most of the projects will only take an hour or less to create.

Working with wire is truly one of the most fulfilling pastimes you will ever embark upon. I hope that *Creative Wire Jewelry* will inspire you to express yourself through wire crafting.

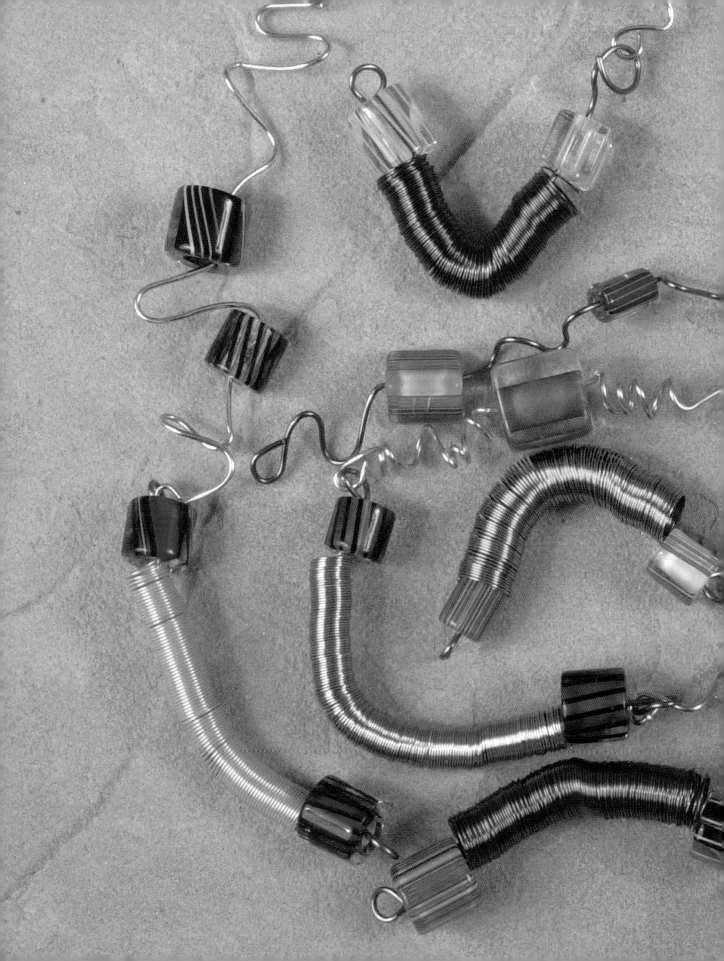

Materials and Supplies

Wire Basics

Making wire jewelry will certainly bring out the designer in you. It's something that, once learned, will never be forgotten. Understanding how wire can work with or against you is something you will discover as you venture into the craft. At first glance, the projects in this book may appear complex, but with a little practice, the right tools, and some basic techniques, you will be well on your way to mastering any of these wonderful designs.

WIRE

Wire is available in different metals, coatings, densities, and shapes. In this book, I will be using three varieties of wires from Artistic Wire, Ltd.: enamel-coated copper wire, enamel-coated silver wire, and brass wire. Costs of wire vary depending upon the metal and the gauge. If you are a beginner wire crafter, it's advisable to practice with a less expensive copper wire of the same gauge rather than costly niobium, silver-, or gold-filled wire.

Wire can be purchased in kits containing twelve 5-yard spools. Individual spools containing 10, 15, 20, and 30 yards of wire are also available. Generally, the heavier the gauge of wire, the less yardage on the spool. For example, 18-gauge

There are a wide variety of wires available, in different metals, colors, and gauges. Beginners can jump-start their collection by purchasing kits containing spools of wires in assorted colors.

spools contain 10 yards of wire; 26-gauge spools hold 30 yards of wire. Most of the projects presented in this book require only 1 to 3 yards of wire.

GAUGE

Gauge refers to the thickness or diameter of the wire, which can range from ultra-fine to very thick. The higher the gauge, the thinner the wire (for example, a 10-gauge wire is much thicker than a 28-gauge wire). The gauge of the wire will affect the appearance of your wire design, as well as dictate how much weight elements of the design can support. For jewelry, 16-, 18-, and 20-gauge wire is most often recommended because of its strength. Thinner wires can be used to create wire bead segments and for wire wrapping (see page 34). Heavier 18- and 20-gauge wire can also be used for wrapping and for making wire beads.

When selecting a gauge, think of how you're going to use the wire. Always remember, if you need strength to support a wire component, use a heavier gauge wire. Although you can combine a heavier gauge link with a lighter gauge wire bead, a light gauge link will most likely not be able to support a heavier gauge component. Two light gauge wires can be twisted together to create one heavier gauge one.

Thinner gauge wire— from 18 to 28 gauge—is very pliable and easy to work with. The wire listed in the materials can be substituted, as long as you use the same thickness, or gauge.

COLOR

Baking approximately 8 to 11 coats of enamel onto copper or silver wire produces colored wire. The color of the base wire will affect the finished color of the baked enamel. Silver base wire will produce a brighter color, while copper base wire will create an earthier tone. For example, green enamel baked onto a copper base will appear darker than the same color baked on a silver base.

Colored wires lend a unique and unexpected look to wire designs. Though using a single color of wire is very classic and traditional, there's no need to limit yourself to a single color—variety is part of the appeal. By combining contrasting or complementary shades of wire, you can give a single design multiple looks. Try twisting several different colored wires together to create a new illusion of color.

When choosing a color scheme, consider what ultimate effect you would like to achieve. Combine analogous colors for a subtle, harmonious look, or high-contrast colors for a bolder and more energetic design. The variety of effects you can achieve by mixing colors is endless. When adding beads to your design, choose colors that complement rather than compete with the wire.

Colored wires add an exciting dimension to any jewelry design. Try twisting several different enamel-coated wires together to create a new illusion of color.

Findings

Findings are the small metal fittings that are used to attach jewelry components to each other, to the body, and to clothing. Examples include jump rings, crimps, clasps, ear wires, hook-and-eye clasps, eyeglass hooks, and eyepins. Both ready-made and self-made findings are included in this book.

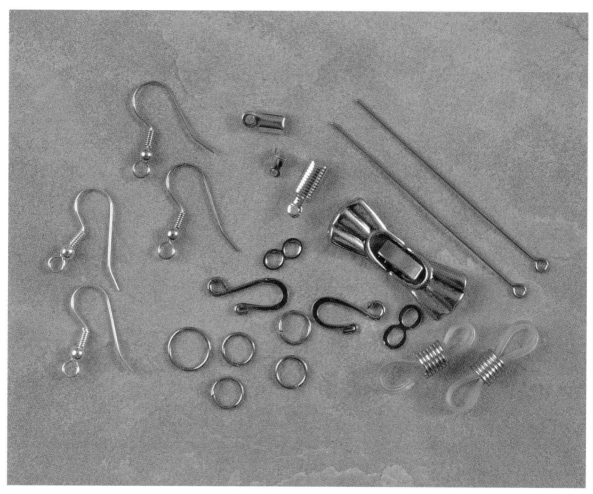

Findings, such as earring hooks, jump rings, eyepins, and clasps, can be bought ready-made from craft stores and specialty suppliers, or self-made from wire.

Tools

There are seven basic tools that I recommend beginners have on hand when starting any of the projects in this book. They are round-nose or needle-nose pliers, flat-nose pliers, tweezer-nose pliers, wire cutters, nylon-jaw pliers, a wire curler, and a jig. Though there are many other tools for wire jewelry making, I recommend that you start with these basics and add more as your proficiency increases. When selecting pliers and cutting tools, look for brands, like Xuron tools, that offer special features like spring-handles. Spring-handles help prevent hand fatigue by opening the tool after it is engaged.

Other essentials to have on hand include a metal file, paper for designing or note taking, a ruler, and small containers for odds and ends. I would also recommend a Wack-it-Down™ or jeweler's hammer and anvil for flattening or texturing wire. You can also texture wire with a paper crimper.

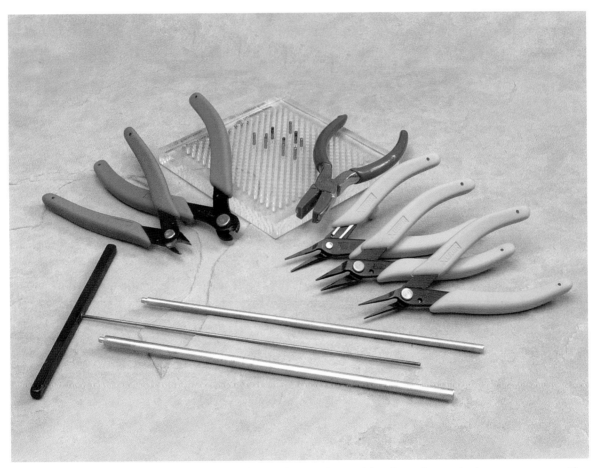

Begin with the essential tools—pliers, cutters, curlers, and jigs. Other useful tools can be acquired as you progress with your skills.

PLIERS

There is nothing more frustrating than trying to create a design when you do not have the appropriate or right-quality pliers to achieve it. I recommend you invest in three pairs of pliers: round- or needle-nose pliers, flat-nose pliers, and tweezer-nose pliers. Round- and needle-nose pliers are essential in creating loops, while flat-nose pliers are used to hold a design firm while shaping the wire. To prevent damaging your wire, look for pliers with smooth jaw edges rather than serrated ones. Nylon-jaw pliers will not mar the wire finish and are ideal for straightening and strengthening wire.

WIRE CUTTERS

A good pair of sharp cutters is essential in wire jewelry making. The gauge of the wire that you wish to cut determines the size and type of the cutter you should use. Xuron makes a good selection of precision cutting tools and is my tool of choice. Angled cutters with fine-pointed ends will help you achieve optimum results creating delicate and intricate jewelry designs. I would recommend using a heavier track cutter for 18- and 16-gauge wires. Use a hard wire cutter for 10-gauge wires. Never use a fine cutter on heavy gauge wires—you will destroy your pliers with one cut.

Wire cutters come in a variety of sizes to cut different thicknesses of wire. Very thin wire can be cut with scissors, but there is a risk of dulling the blades.

WIRE CURLERS

The most basic wire-curling tool is a mandrel, which is a long metal rod available in various diameters. Wire can be manually twisted around a mandrel to create loose coils. In addition, there are wire curlers that have handles that help twist the wire around a mandrel. These wire curlers are much easier to use than any manual model, and will always produce better results. If a wire curler is not available, wire can be twisted around a dowel or round-nose pliers to create large- to medium-sized coils. For smaller, more intricate coils, wrap wire around an embroidery, tapestry, or smaller needle.

In this book I use two basic wire curlers: the Deluxe Version Twist 'n' Curl™ and the Wire Worker™. These wire curlers include a selection of large to small mandrels that can be easily changed to create various-sized coils and beads. Each tool essentially does the same work, but varies slightly in mandrel diameter, shape, and length.

JIGS

A jig is a tool that uses pegs to bend and shape wire repetitively and precisely. There are several jigs on the market, some with repositionable pegs and others with fixed pegs. The Olympus WigJig™ is a transparent version with movable pegs. The see-through peg board allows you to replicate patterns placed beneath it. The Jewelry Jig™ is the craft version of the WigJig™. It performs the same

Wire curlers make it easy to create large- and small-sized wire coils and beads.

functions as the WigJig™ but is made of lightweight plastic. If a commercial jig is not available, you can make your own simply by drilling holes in a piece of wood, then inserting nails with the nail heads removed.

FILES

To prevent snags or scratches, use a metal file to remove burrs or sharp edges from cut wire. Small metal files, or needle files, have different shapes and cuts, from coarse to fine. The teeth on the files can only cut on the forward stroke, thus the files should be lifted on the backward movement.

EXTRAS

The supplies you will need to create the designs in this book will vary from project to project; however, I recommend you always have on hand a variety of different colors and sizes of beads, sea glass, wire mesh, leather lace, ribbons, cording, double-faced super-sticky tape, and special glues.

When gluing wire, use metal glues to secure metal to metal, and a clear-drying jewelry glue, such as Beacon's Gem-Tac™ glue, to secure wire to beads and stones.

Wire mesh comes in a variety of colors and gauges. The number on the mesh denotes the number of holes per inch. For jewelry making, choose higher-numbered mesh, which is finer and made of thinner wire.

Jigs, available in different weights and sizes, are peg boards used to loop and shape wire.

Getting Organized

Though there are probably dozens of ways to organize your wire stash, I prefer to organize my wire by gauge, color, and type of metal. For instance, I group all of my copper enamel-coated wire spools in one drawer. I then sub-group the wires by color and gauge. I also group the gauges and colors of all my silver enamel-coated wires and plastic-coated wire in the same fashion.

To organize my beads, I separate them by color and store them in clear cases. When working, I place the beads in front of me on a folded towel. The towel prevents the beads from rolling and shifting as I thread them on wire. The pile of the towel anchors the beads, allowing me to keep them in organized groups.

I like to keep my tools in a drawer close to my wire and beads. While at my work table, I lay all of my tools in front of my workspace for quick access. I also use tools with handles in different colors for easy recognition.

Group wire spools by color and gauge for quick access and easy recognition.

Good Work Habits

When I'm teaching someone to work with wire I always promote safety. When cutting wire, it's extremely important to contain or hold the loose ends so that they do not become projectiles. Safety glasses for eye protection should be used so that small pieces of wire do not injure your eyes or the eyes of others near you. Keep a pair of safety glasses with your other tools so that they will always be on hand. Also, prevent wrist stress and hand fatigue by bending the wire—not your wrists. Whenever possible, limit the range of wrist movement. Wristbands can be worn to help prevent injury. If your hand becomes tired, take a moment to rest before continuing. Lastly, always keep small pieces of wire and beads stored safely out of the reach of small children.

To avoid wrist strain and hand fatigue, grasp and bend the wire with pliers using limited wrist movement.

Design Basics

Essential Techniques

Making wire jewelry can be easy once you master a few basic and simple techniques.

WORKING OFF THE SPOOL

In most cases, you will work off the spool before cutting the wire. To prevent waste, cut the wire only when stated in the instructions. This will save you from cutting the wire too long or too short.

HARDENING THE WIRE

Many professional jewelers harden the wire before crafting to help it retain its shape. This is an optional first step that you may choose to take, as you become more serious about your jewelry designs. Hardening the wire can be accomplished in several different ways. First, you can use two pliers to grasp the ends of a loose piece of wire, then flex the wire back and forth up to six times. While this is a simple approach, you should bear in mind that if you bend the wire too far or too much, breakage can occur. Other hardening methods include pressing on the wire or pulling and straightening it with nylon-jaw pliers before shaping, or pounding on the finished wire design with a rubber mallet or jeweler's hammer. While my preference is using nylon-jaw pliers, practice and experience will determine the best hardening method for you.

WIRE TAIL

The tail of the wire is the very end of the working wire. The length of the tail will vary with each design. The tail will usually need to be tucked into the design to lock the wire into place and to create a nice finish.

TWISTING WIRE

Wires are sometimes twisted together to finish off a design. This can be accomplished by holding the ends of two or more wires together with flat-nose or nylon-jaw pliers, then turning the pliers to twist the wires. For more lengthy twists of wire, cut two equal lengths of wire, fold them in the middle, and secure the wire ends in a vise. Fasten a hooked piece of wire in a hand drill, and hook it to the bend of the secured wires. Turn the hand drill to twist the wires together.

Jewelry Components and Links

Most of the findings or components you will be making are common "links" for many of the designs in this book. With a little practice, and wire bending skills, you can create your own professional-looking links.

LOOPS

Loops are used to connect jewelry components and findings. A loop is made by holding the wire flush with the round nose of the pliers, then bending the end of the wire over the pliers. The size of the loop will depend upon the positioning of the wire onto the nose of the pliers. Position the wire at the tip of the nose to make small-sized loops. Place the wire further up the nose to make larger loops.

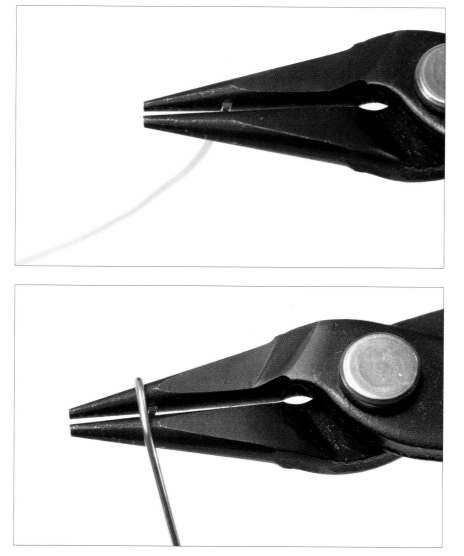

1 Use round-nose pliers to shape wire into a loop. Working off the spool, hold the end of the wire flush with the edge of the pliers.

2 Bring the wire up and over the pliers full circle to form a loop.

To make a bail, wrap the wire twice around a dowel or other cylindrical object, then secure the bail by wrapping the tail around the base of the wire.

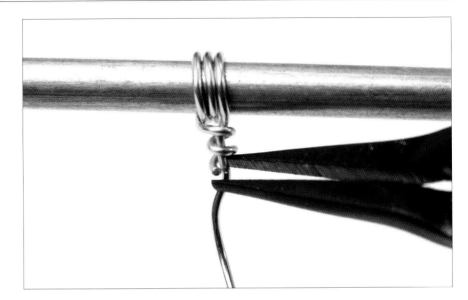

BAILS

Similar to loops, bails are used for supporting pendants and other jewelry components. They are usually made from the wire existing on the jewelry design.

EYE PINS OR BEAD LINKS

Use 18- or 20-gauge wire to make a bead link. Cut the wire the total length of the bead or beads you plan to thread on the link, plus $1/2$ to $3/4$ inch. Using round-nose pliers, grip the wire approximately $3/8$ inch from the end and bend the wire into a right angle with the short end of the wire against the side of the pliers; close the loop. Slide a bead onto the wire and make a second loop against the bead at the opposite end of the wire. Tighten any gaps in the loops after linking components.

Make a bead link working off the spool. Thread the bead or beads onto the wire and loop the end of the wire. Loop the wire against the bead at the opposite end, then cut the wire.

HOOK-AND-EYE CLASPS

Hook-and-eye clasps are used to fasten necklace chains and bracelets. There are a variety of types of hook-and-eye fasteners to choose from—select the style that best suits your jewelry design. The hooks and eyes can be made from loose pieces of wire and joined to the jewelry item, or formed directly from the working wire.

There are two techniques I use to make eye clasps. One is worked from the spool, while the other uses the existing wire or wires from the design. Each technique will give you a completely different-looking clasp. When working from the spool, loop the end of 18- or 20-gauge wire, then bring the wire up and over your round-nose pliers, leaving a minimum of $1/2$ inch between the loop and the bend. Bend the wire down the pliers and make an equal-sized loop at the opposite end of the wire. Cut the wire, cross the two loops over each other, and secure the loops with a jump ring.

The second technique I use for making an eye clasp is worked from the existing wire on a design piece for a built-in look. I use a mandrel or dowel to form a circle at the end of my design, then wrap the tail around the base of the circle. This is very similar to making a bail (see page 26).

To make an oblong eye clasp (pictured with spiral clasp, page 28), cut a 1½-inch length of 18- to 20-gauge wire and bend the wire at the center. Loop both ends of the wire. Connect the loops to a jump ring or other link.

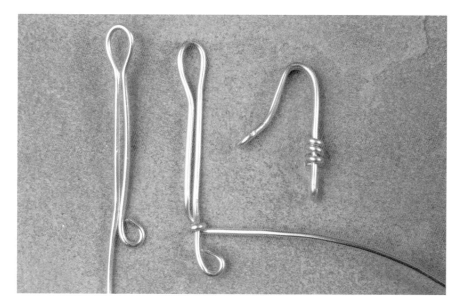

Hook-and-loop fasteners provide a neat finish to any style bracelet or necklace.

Eye clasps can be made from loose pieces of wire and joined to a design, or made from the existing wire, as shown.

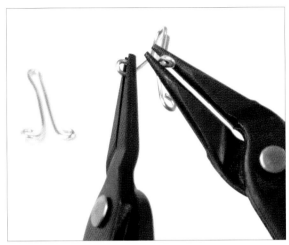

To make a hook, cut a 4-inch length of 18- or 20-gauge wire. Bend the wire approximately 1¼ inches over round-nose pliers and gently press the wires together at the bend. Keeping the short wire away and the long wire closest to you, form a loop at the base of the short wire and wrap the long end around both wires two or three times. Cut and tuck the long wire end, then bend the hook at the center over round-nose pliers to complete.

For another variation of hook, begin with a 1½-inch length of 18- or 20- gauge wire (longer for a larger hook). Loop each end of the wire to make a hairpin, then bend at the center of the wire using a mandrel or other round object, such as round-nose pliers. Hold the hook in place with flat-nose pliers and fold the bended portion over and down to the loops.

To make a spiral-style hook, begin with a 4-inch length of wire and spiral one end. Loop the opposite end to join the hook to the jewelry item. For a built-in hook, simply spiral the wire existing on the design.

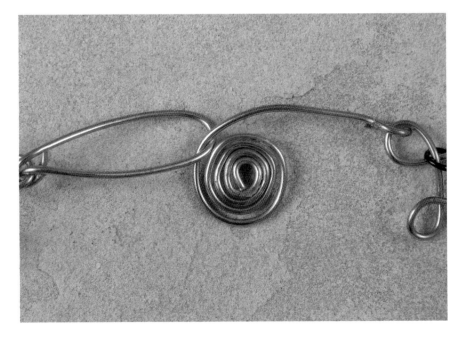

S-HOOKS

To form an S-hook, working from the spool, loop one end of 18- or 20-gauge wire. Make a second loop in the opposite direction by turning the pliers toward you. Cut off the excess wire from the spool at the center of the crossbar.

JUMP RINGS

Jump rings are circles of wire of varying sizes that are used to connect short links. To make a large jump ring, twist a length of 18- or 20-gauge wire around a dowel and cut the coils. You can also use the Twist 'n' Curl™ to make jump rings of various sizes. Simply coil the wire around the mandrel, slip the coil off, then cut up one side of the coil with wire cutters to free the rings.

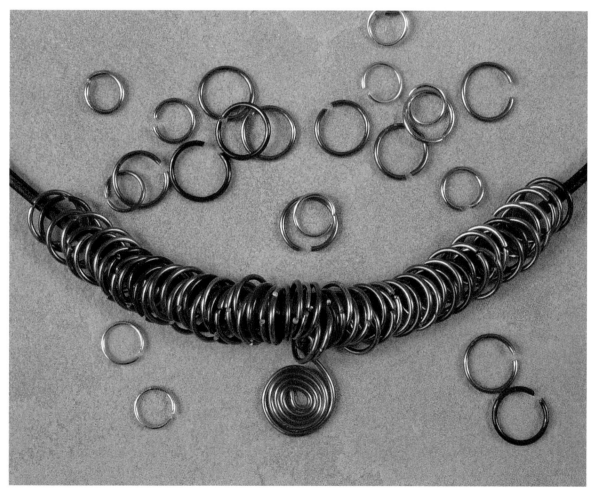

Jump rings, used to link components, are infinitely useful in wire jewelry making.

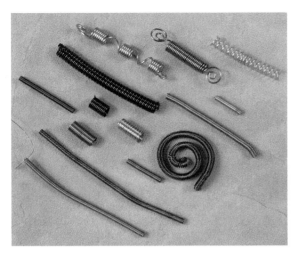

COILS

A coil can be made by using a wire curler or by wrapping wire around a tapestry, embroidery, or smaller needle, a dowel, or other cylindrical object. Coiled wire can be shaped and added to other components to create numerous design effects. Coil multiple colors of wire together to make double- and triple-wire coils. Beaded wire can also be coiled for a variety of stunning looks.

SPIRALS

To shape wire into a spiral, first loop the end of the wire with round-nose pliers. Pinch the wire between your index finger and thumb (or use a flat-nose pliers to hold in place) and spiral clockwise. Vary the tension of the spiral to create a tighter or looser look. A double spiral is made in the same manner as a single spiral, except instead of one you make two equal-sized coils that meet at the center of the wire. A reverse spiral uses the same technique as a double spiral, except the spirals are twisted in opposite directions.

WIGGLES

Wiggle describes when wire is wound loosely back and forth. Wiggles can be made as tight or loose, regular or irregular as desired. Use round-nose pliers to shape wire into wiggles. A jig can also be used to create wiggles.

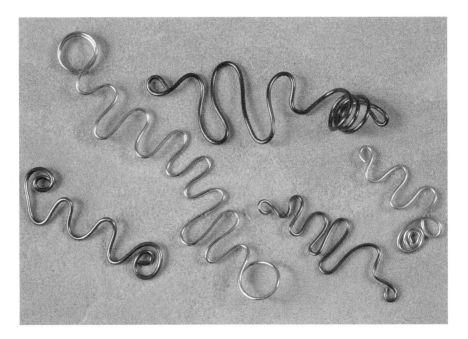

Jig Design

When making multiple wire links, you will want to use a jig. This time-saving tool is essential for making repetitive and precise shapes. Using a jig involves simply placing pegs in a specific pattern on a baseboard, then looping wire around the pegs. The look of the finished link is determined by the direction in which the wire is moved around the pegs. A clear jig, like the one used for the projects in this book, allows the user to position a pattern under the jig to guide peg placement.

To design with a jig, loop the end of the wire and position the loop over the first peg. Wind the wire around the pegs following a pattern, or as desired. When you come to the last peg, remove the link from the jig and cut the wire flush to make a closed loop at the opposite end of the link. Experiment with different peg placements and wire gauges to create your own unique designs.

Jigs are essential tools in jewelry design. By wrapping wire around the jig pegs, you can create multiple links in identical shapes and patterns.

Wire Bead Making

Wire beads? You bet! Wire curling tools make them easy to create. Simply coil the wire, then coil the wire again to make different size and shape beads. The length of your coil and the gauge and tension of the wire will determine the size and look of your finished bead. When creating wire beads, always work from the spool of the wire.

Wire beads are fun and easy to make. With the wide assortment of wires and beads available, you can create an infinite number of wire beads in a variety of shapes and sizes.

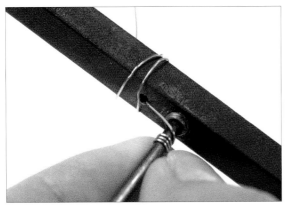

1 The first step to making wire beads is coiling the wire. Thread the wire into the hole in the handle of the Twist 'n' Curl™, allowing for a 2- to 3-inch long tail. Wrap the tail around the handle to secure the wire. Hold the handle vertically with the wire up, over the mandrel and between yourself and the mandrel. Secure the wire between your index finger and thumb, then twist the handle and wire using your opposite hand.

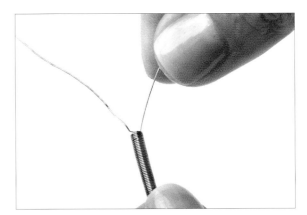

2 Cut the wire on the long end of the coil and remove the coil from the mandrel. Thread a wire through the cut end of the coil and bring the tail through to meet the coil's tail. Secure the new wire to the handle as in step 1, and coil four or more times around the mandrel.

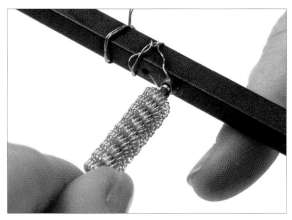

3 Slide the coil up the wire and against the mandrel and secure the tail to the handle. Push the coil firmly against the mandrel and begin wrapping the coil until it is completely wrapped around the mandrel. Coil the wire from the spool 4 or more times around the mandrel. Make sure both ends of the coil bead are equal. Cut the wires at both ends and remove the bead from the mandrel.

For a variation, add seed beads to the wire before coiling, then follow steps 2 and 3 for making a wire bead. The resulting beads, referred to as wire seed beads, can be made large or small in single or multiple colors, as desired.

To make a chubby bead, make a coil the length of the mandrel following step 1. Follow steps 2 and 3, only leave a 2- or 3-inch tail at one end of the bead. Thread another wire through the wire bead and curl the wire bead using loose but equal tension.

Wire Wrapping

Wire wrapping broken stained glass was how I began my wire-crafting career. It was simple to do, yet gave a whole new dimension to something plain and ordinary. Everything from beads, to glass, to wire mesh can be decoratively wrapped with wire. The wire can be wrapped in even rows, or in a random manner—it can even be neatly spiraled and wrapped for stunning results. In addition to objects, wire can be wrapped and twisted around itself to create changes in color and texture.

When wrapping beads, glass, wire mesh, or flat objects, leave at least a 2-inch tail at the beginning and end of each wrapped piece. The key to successful wrapping is always to press the wire against the object with each wrap to ensure stability. Twist and tuck your wire tails together to enclose the piece, or leave longer tails to shape into links.

Almost anything can be wrapped with wire. The best technique to use will depend upon the element you wish to wrap and the look you desire.

MESH BEADS

Mesh beads make stunning jewelry components, whether dangling from earrings and chains, or incorporated in bracelets and hair accessories. To make a mesh

bead, press a piece of mesh flat or wrap it around a mandrel. Then, wrap the mesh with wire in neat, orderly rows, or randomly criss-cross the wire a few or several times around the mesh until it is secured. For further embellishment, beads can be laced on the wire before wrapping.

WIRE-WRAPPED GLASS

Wire-wrap ordinary glass pieces to create dazzling and colorful beads. To avoid injury, never use rough-cut glass for wire-wrapping. Instead, look for smooth-edged glass, such as sea glass, heat-treated, and tumbled glass, all readily available in craft and hobby stores.

WIRE-WRAPPED BEADS

Wire-wrapping adds a new dimension to commercially made beads. Almost any bead can be wire-wrapped, as long as the ends are secured to ensure closure. Wire-wrap donut-shaped beads for pendants or earrings. Spiral or simply wind wire around larger beads to enliven them with texture and color.

Simply by cutting, folding, or rolling wire mesh and wrapping it with wire, you can create an array of unique-looking beads of incredible depth and texture.

Bracelets

Twiggy Bracelet

This design was inspired by the twiggy-branch wire trees that were so popular in the 1960s and '70s. I've updated the simple technique with new wire colors to create this chic and contemporary-looking bracelet.

SKILL LEVEL
Intermediate

WHAT YOU'LL NEED

Wire

Colored silver wire
28-gauge Blue

Materials
Hook-and-eye clasp

Tools
Round- and flat-nose
    pliers
Wire cutters
Metal file

Beads
Fifty to fifty-five $1/4$-inch
    round glass beads,
    blue and clear

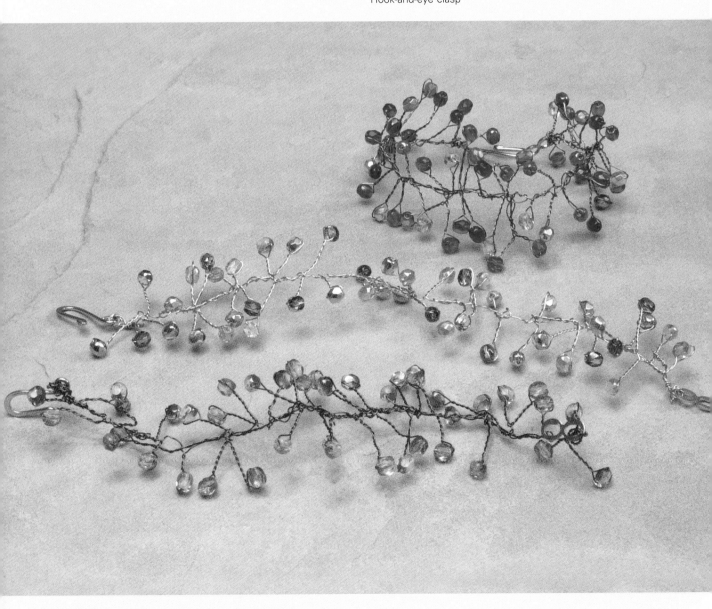

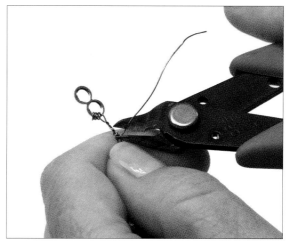

1 *Thread 50 to 55 blue and clear beads onto the wire in random order.*

2 *Secure the end of the wire to the eye finding by wrapping through the hole several times. Cut the wire and file the end as needed.*

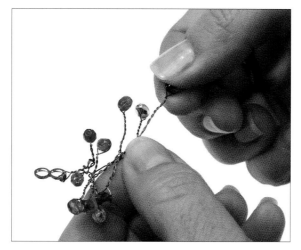

3 *Working with one bead at a time, slide a bead out approximately ¹/₂ inch from the eye finding. Hold the bead firmly between your fingers, then twist the wire until it meets the base of the finding. Repeat at the opposite side of the first twist, sliding a bead out ¹/₂ inch, then doubling and twisting the wire.*

4 *Move up the wire approximately ¹/₂ inch, twist the wire, then repeat step 3. Make the bracelet to your wrist size plus ¹/₂ inch for ease. Cut the wire from the spool, leaving a 2-inch tail. Wrap the tail through the hook finding and secure the wire with flat-nose pliers.*

Classic Wire Bracelet

Silver wire combined with gold or brass tones always looks lovely. Though this bracelet is rather simple to create, the end result is truly fashionable and elegant.

SKILL LEVEL
Intermediate

WHAT YOU'LL NEED

Wire

Silver wire
20-gauge Silver

Brass wire
20-gauge Non-Tarnishing
   Brass

Tools
Round- and flat-nose
   pliers
Wire cutters
Wire Worker™

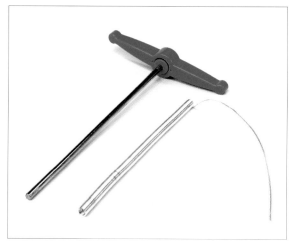

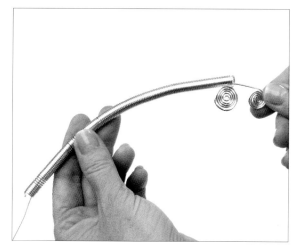

1 Using the largest metal mandrel of the Wire Worker™ and silver wire, make one long coil to wrist size plus 1/2 inch for ease. Cut the wire from the spool, leaving one 2 1/2-inch tail.

2 Spiral the tail on the coil. Insert the silver wire through the coil and spiral the end of the wire. Cut the wire from the spool, leaving an approximately 1 1/2-inch tail; spiral the tail.

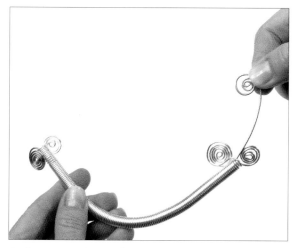

3 Repeat step 2 using brass wire.

4 Fasten the bracelet by overlapping two or more spirals to make a clasp.

Colorful Coil Bracelet

Wire seed bead coils combined with heavier gauge wires create an icy blue illusion. I've combined similarly colored wire and beads to make this delicate-looking bracelet.

SKILL LEVEL
Challenging

WHAT YOU'LL NEED

Wire

Colored silver wire
22-gauge Silver
20-gauge Silver
20-gauge Ice Blue

Beads
Two hundred seed beads, blue

Tools
Round- and flat-nose pliers
Wire cutters
Twist 'n' Curl™

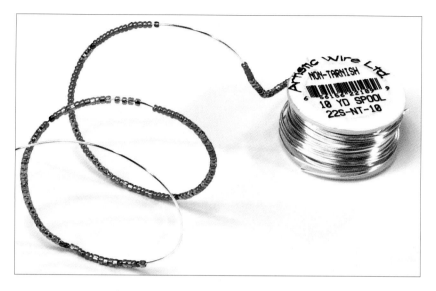

1 Working off the spool, thread approximately 10 inches' worth of beads onto 22-gauge silver wire.

2 Using the smallest mandrel from the Twist 'n' Curl™, secure the 20-gauge blue and silver wires and the beaded wire and make a coil to wrist size. (Alternatively, you can use several colors of seed beads threaded onto three wires for a different effect.)

3 Thread the 20-gauge silver wire through the coil. Cut the wire from the spool, leaving 4-inch tails on each end. Using pliers, form the ends into a hook-and-eye clasp (see page 27).

Bountiful Wire Bracelet

Free-form jewelry making is fun and very easy to do. This simple yet elegant combination of wire and beads creates a wonderful, abstract design that is suitable for both day and evening wear.

SKILL LEVEL
Intermediate

WHAT YOU'LL NEED

Wire

Colored silver wire
24-gauge Gold
20-gauge Non-Tarnishing
    Silver

Beads
Two hundred seed beads,
    silver
Ten 1/4-inch glass beads,
    two-tone gray/gold

Tools
Round- and flat-nose
    pliers
Wire cutters

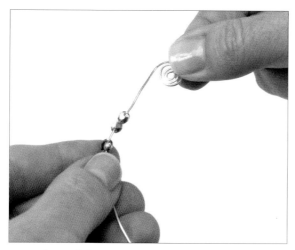

1   *Working off the spool, thread ten glass beads onto the 20-gauge wire. Spiral the end of the wire to create a hook.*

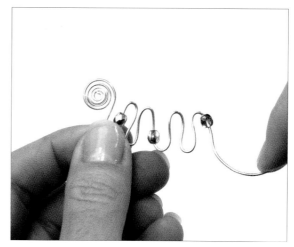

2   *Bend the wire in a zigzag fashion, making the bends no more than ¹/₂ inch in width and spacing beads onto every second or third bend. Zigzag to fit wrist plus ¹/₂ inch for ease. Cut the wire, leaving an approximately 1¹/₂-inch tail; spiral the tail.*

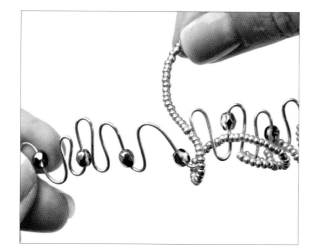

3   *Thread 30 inches' worth of seed beads onto the gold wire. Secure the tail of the beaded wire to one end of the bracelet. Weave the beaded wire over and under the bends in the bracelet. Cut the beaded wire from the spool, leaving a 2-inch tail. Secure the tail to the spirals on the bracelet. (Note: You may add additional beads if desired. This can be accomplished by repeating this step.)*

4   *Make an oblong clasp to fit the size of the spiral hook (see page 27). Attach the clasp to one end of the bracelet by looping the clasp ends and securing them to the spiral.*

Wire Watchband

Keep time with a handsome beaded wire watchband. This unique and unusual accessory will complement most any style of wristwatch.

SKILL LEVEL
Challenging

WHAT YOU'LL NEED

Wire

Colored copper wire
22-gauge Dark Green
20-gauge Dark Green

Brass wire
22-gauge Non-Tarnishing Brass

Materials
Wristwatch
Fold-over clasps

Beads
112 seed beads, gold
Sixteen $1/8$-inch glass cut beads, burgundy

Tools
Round- and flat-nose pliers
Wire cutters
Twist 'n' Curl™

1 Cut four 7-inch lengths of 20-gauge wire. Attach the wires to the watch by looping the ends and securing them to the outside openings on the watch face.

2 Using the smallest mandrel of the Twist 'n' Curl™, make ten ³/₈-inch coils each from the 22-gauge brass and green wires. Use 22-gauge wire to make eyepins for each coil and for eighteen bead components (38 total). Loop the ends of the pins with pliers to secure the beads and coils.

3 Thread the components onto the wristband wires, alternating coiled and beaded pins and separating each component with seed beads.

4 Attach a clasp to each end of the wristband and secure with pliers.

Pendants

Purple and Pink Pendant

Square-shaped beads can be used in lots of imaginative ways. The lovely glass bead that serves as the focal point of this pendant gave inspiration to the other design elements.

SKILL LEVEL
Challenging

WHAT YOU'LL NEED

Wire

Colored copper wire
18-gauge Natural
22-gauge Natural

Colored silver wire
28-gauge Plum

Materials
One yard of 1/8-inch leather lace

Beads
One 1/2- to 3/4-inch flat glass bead, pink iridescent
Four 1/4-inch glass beads, lavender/copper iridescent
One 1/2-inch glass leaf bead, copper/pink iridescent
Five 1/8-inch glass seed beads, lavender iridescent

Tools
Twist 'n' Curl ™
Round-nose pliers
Nylon-grip pliers
Wire cutters

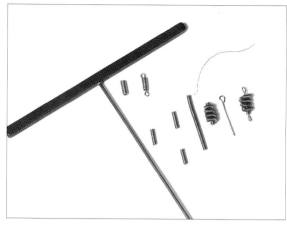

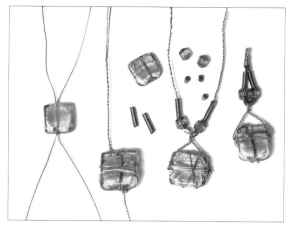

1 Using the smallest mandrel of the Twist 'n' Curl ™ and the 28-gauge wire, make three ³/₈-inch coils and one 1¹/₂-inch coil. Twist the longest coil into a wire bead (see page 32), then thread one 1¹/₄-inch 18-gauge wire eyepin through the center of the bead. Loop the opposite end of the eyepin. Using the curling tool and 18-gauge wire, make one ³/₈-inch coil. With pliers, lift and turn out a loop on each end of the wire coil.

2 Cut two 20-inch lengths of 22-gauge wire. Thread both wires through the flat bead. Wrap both wires around the bead until it is secure, leaving at least 4-inch tails. Twist each pair of wire tails together (see page 24). Twist the twisted wires together two or three times until secure. Separate the tails and thread onto each in order: ¹/₈-inch seed bead, ¹/₄-inch glass bead, ³/₈-inch wire coil, and ¹/₄-inch glass bead. Twist the tails together again, and thread one ¹/₈-inch seed bead on the joined wires. Create a hook from the remaining wire and cut off the excess.

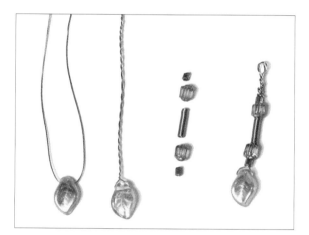

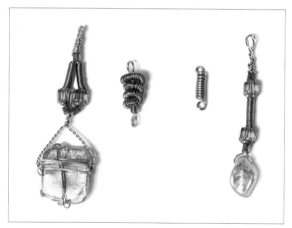

3 Cut a 10-inch length of 22-gauge wire and thread it through the leaf bead, centering the bead. Twist the tails, then thread onto the twisted wire in order: ¹/₈-inch seed bead, ¹/₄-inch glass bead, ³/₈-inch wire coil, ¹/₄-inch glass bead, and ¹/₈-inch seed bead. Loop the twisted wire to create a hook. Wrap the remaining wire around the base of the hook and cut off the excess.

4 Using round-nose pliers, connect the pendant components in the order as shown. Hang the pendant from leather lace or cord.

Six-Tier Wire Coil Pendant

Glass beads, wire beads, and coils combine to create this eye-catching pendant. Apply the same technique with different wires and beads to make pendants in a wide array of styles.

SKILL LEVEL
Intermediate

WHAT YOU'LL NEED

Wire

Colored copper wire
22-gauge Non-Tarnishing Brass
24-gauge Gun Metal
20-gauge Gun Metal

Materials
One yard of ⅛-inch leather lace

Beads
Fourteen ¼-inch glass beads, brown/copper

Thirteen seed beads, brown, silver, and gold

Tools
Twist 'n' Curl™
Round- and flat-nose pliers
Wire cutters

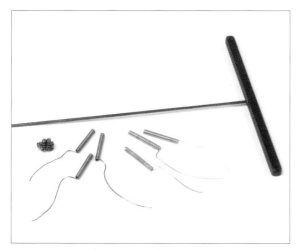

1 *Using the smallest mandrel on the Twist 'n' Curl™ and 22- and 24-gauge wires, make three equal-length coils (approximately 1-inch long or less) in each gauge of wire. Thread the 22-gauge core wire through the 24-gauge coils and make three wire beads (see page 32).*

2 *Using 20-gauge wire, make seven 1-inch eyepins and two 1½-inch eyepins. Thread a glass bead, a coil or wire bead, and another glass bead onto six of the 1-inch eyepins. Loop the eyepin ends to secure the beads. On the remaining 1-inch eyepin, thread seed and glass beads as shown, hanging a coil and bead component from the center.*

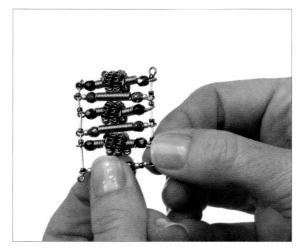

3 *Connect the components with the two 1½-inch eyepins, alternating coil and wire bead components and separating each with a seed bead. Attach the beaded and hanging component last and loop the ends of the eyepins to secure.*

4 *Make a ¼-inch 20-gauge spiral and loop the end to secure it to the bottom of the hanging component. Thread leather lace through the top holes of the pendant.*

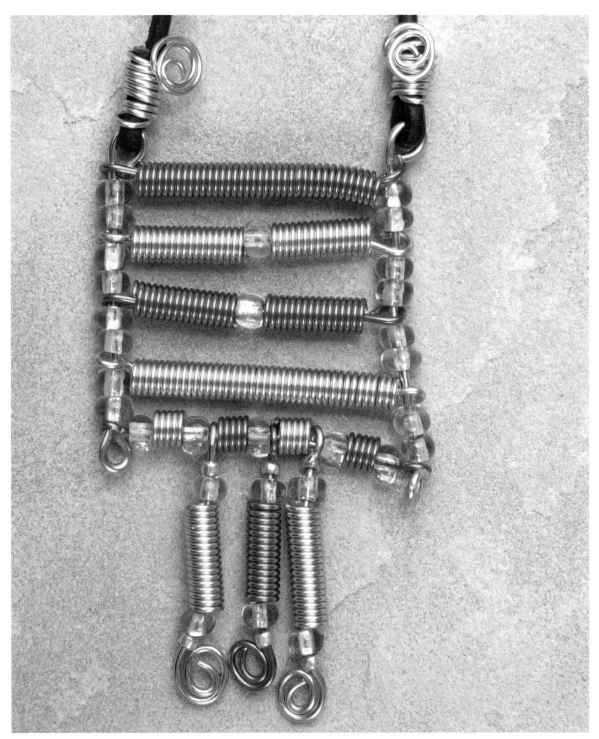

ALTERNATE SIX-TIER PENDANT

For a different look, instead of adding wire beads, make the pendant using only wire coils. Combine colored wires in light and dark shades to give the pendant a contemporary appeal.

Double Wire Bead Pendant

Your friends will marvel at this 3-D pendant. Alternate or combine additional colors of wire and beads to create a variety of looks.

SKILL LEVEL
Challenging

WHAT YOU'LL NEED

Wire

Colored silver wire
28-gauge Peacock Blue
28-gauge Seafoam Green
20-gauge Seafoam Green

Colored copper wire
22-gauge Black
20-gauge Black

Materials
One yard of ¼-inch satin ribbon

Beads
Fifty seed beads, blue/black iridescent

One ³/₈-inch round glass bead, aqua
One ½-inch leaf bead, aqua iridescent

Tools
Round- and flat-nose pliers
Wire cutters
Twist 'n' Curl™

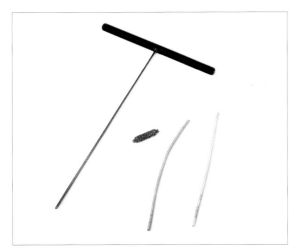

1 *Using the smallest mandrel of Twist 'n' Curl™, make one 5-inch coil each from the green and blue 28-gauge wires. Make one ½- to 1-inch wire seed bead from 22-gauge black wire (see page 33).*

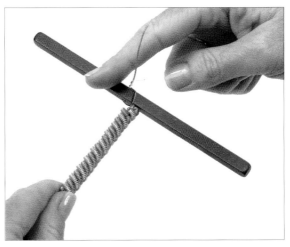

2 *Thread matching wire through the long coils and twist the coils together to make a double wire bead.*

3 *Thread the 20-gauge green wire through the double wire bead and twist the wires to make a chubby wire bead (see page 33).*

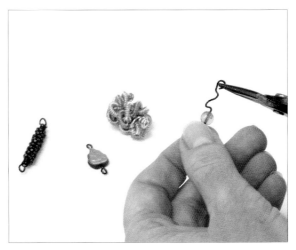

4 *Using the 20-gauge black copper wire, make eyepins for the two wire beads and the leaf bead. For the aqua bead, loop the end of a 1¼-inch length of 20-gauge wire. Thread the bead onto the wire, then make wiggles in the wire and loop the opposite end.*

5 *Connect all of the components as shown and hang the pendant from ribbon.*

ALTERNATE DOUBLE WIRE BEAD PENDANTS

Make four wire beads using wires and lengths as indicated in steps 1–3 above. Thread alternating glass and wire beads onto 20-gauge wire. Coil the beaded wire to create a long wire and bead component. Make a 20-gauge wire eyepin the length of the component and thread it through the entire bead. Add teardrop and glass beads to 22-gauge black wire. Loop and secure the wire at the top of the glass bead and attach to the bottom of the component.

Make one wire seed bead using 150 to 200 seed beads. Make a 20-gauge eyepin the length of the bead and thread the eyepin through the bead. Wire-wrap a flat bead or shell, then add additional beads to the wire ends. Loop the wire ends and connect all of the components.

Wire-Wrapped Glass and Bead Pendant

Consumer-friendly glass, such as sea glass or other treated glass, is a great element to incorporate in wire jewelry. Let the intriguing shapes and translucent colors of the glass inspire your creativity.

SKILL LEVEL
Beginner

WHAT YOU'LL NEED

Wire

Colored copper wire
24-gauge Natural

Materials
One yard of $1/4$-inch leather lace or $1/4$-inch satin ribbon

Beads
One 2-inch piece of sea glass (or other consumer-friendly glass)
Eleven assorted $1/4$- to $3/8$-inch glass beads, brown and amber

Tools
Round-nose pliers
Wire cutters

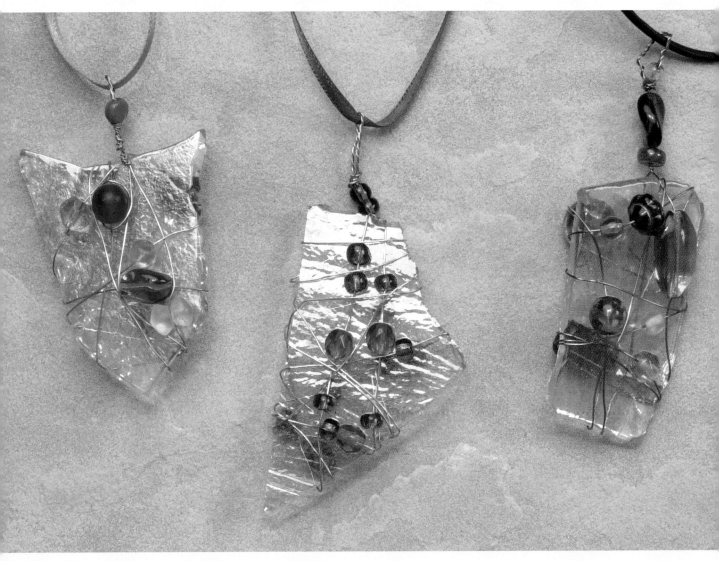

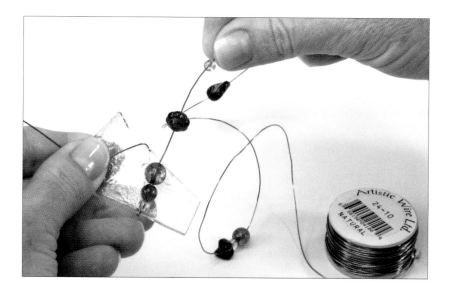

1 Working off the spool, thread all of the beads onto the 24-gauge wire. Leaving a 3-inch tail, wrap the glass piece with the beaded wire, spacing the beads as desired. With each wrap, press the wire firmly against the glass.

2 When the glass is completely wrapped, cut the wire from the spool, leaving a 3-inch tail.

3 Twist the tails together, then thread two beads onto the twisted wire. From the twisted wire, create a loop for hanging, then twist and tuck in the wire ends to secure. Hang the pendant from leather lace or ribbon.

Spiral Pendant

Make a bold and beautiful statement using heavy-gauge wires. This simple yet elegant wire pendant combines two gauges of wire for added depth and texture.

SKILL LEVEL
Intermediate

WHAT YOU'LL NEED

Wire

Colored copper wire
10-gauge Tinned Copper
22-gauge Tinned Copper

Materials
1/4-inch jump ring
One yard of 1/8-inch leather lace
Beacon's Gem-Tac Glue™

Beads
One 5/8-inch flat-bottom cabochon, blue

Tools
Round- and flat-nose pliers
Wire cutters

1 With cutters, cut five 1¹/₂-inch pieces and one 3¹/₂-inch piece of 22-gauge wire. Form the wire pieces into six double spirals (see page 30).

2 Cut an 8-inch length of 10-gauge wire. With pliers, spiral one end of the wire, then loop the opposite end. (The spiral should measure approximately 1 inch in diameter.)

3 To make a bail, loop the center of a 6¹/₂-inch length of 22-gauge wire and attach one wire end onto the 10-gauge wire spiral. Secure the bail by twisting and wrapping the wire ends below the loops as shown. Form the wire ends into two inverted spirals at the top and bottom of the twist.

4 Glue the cabochon and wire spirals onto the 10–gauge spiral as shown and let dry. Add a jump ring onto the bail and hang the pendant from leather lace.

Stunning Glass Pendant

Simple techniques can produce spectacular effects. Here, wire is wrapped, beaded, and spiraled to create a trio of eye-catching pendants.

SKILL LEVEL
Intermediate

WHAT YOU'LL NEED

Wire

Brass wire
22-gauge Non-Tarnishing Brass
18-gauge Non-Tarnishing Brass

Colored silver wire
28-gauge Blue

Materials
One yard of ¹/₂-inch satin ribbon

Beads
Six ¹/₄- to ¹/₈-inch round glass beads, blue and gold

One ³/₄-inch round glass bead, blue
One ⁵/₈-inch glass or novelty bead

Tools
Round- and flat-nose pliers
Wire cutters
Twist 'n' Curl™

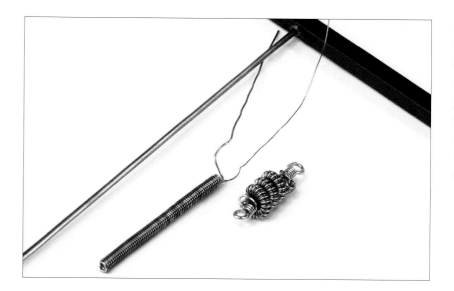

1 Using the smallest mandrel of the Twist 'n' Curl™ and 22- and 28-gauge wires, make a ³/₄-inch double wire bead (see page 32). Using the 18-gauge wire, make a ¹/₄-inch eyepin and thread the eyepin through the wire bead. Loop the wire ends to secure the bead.

2 Thread the glass beads onto the 18-gauge wire in the order shown. Loop the wire end to secure the beads. Cut the wire from the spool, leaving a 2-inch tail.

3 Loop and spiral the wire tail, then position the spiral on top of the large round bead. Wrap the wire around the bead and press. Cut a 3-inch length of 18-gauge wire and spiral one end. Press the spiral onto the front of the large round bead and wrap the wire around the bead. Secure the tail by looping the end and pressing it to the back of the bead. Join the components as shown and hang the pendant from ribbon.

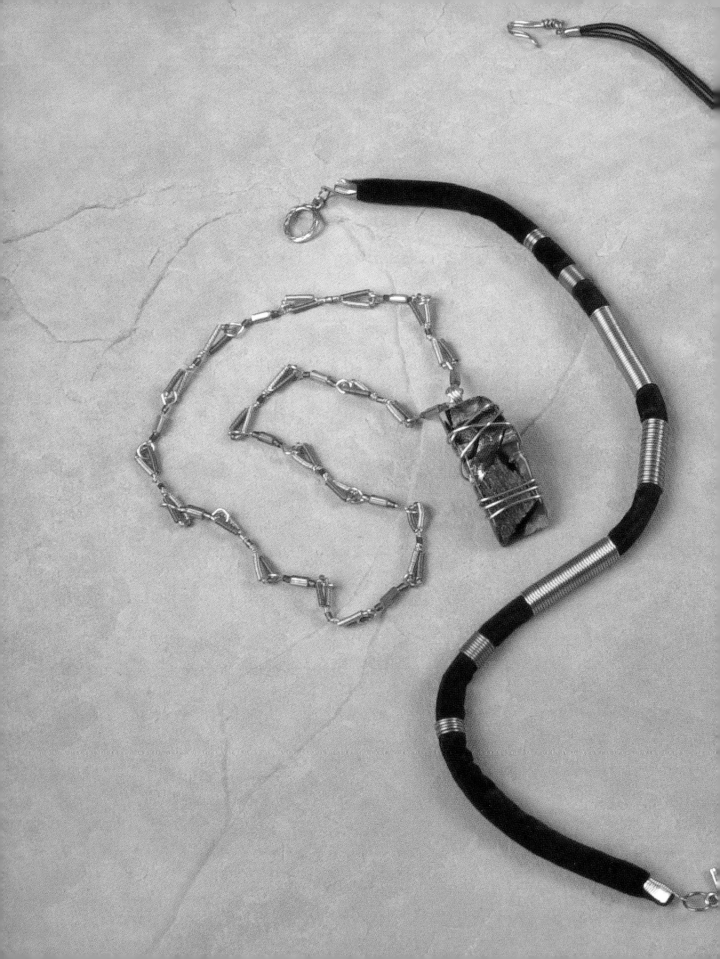

Necklaces, Chains, and Chokers

Coil Choker

This is one of my favorite designs in this book, perhaps because the color and texture of the wire really pops out against the soft, black velvet cording. This choker can be worn for both casual and dressy occasions.

SKILL LEVEL
Beginner

WHAT YOU'LL NEED

Wire

Colored silver wire
20-gauge Peach
20-gauge Fuchsia

Materials
Black velvet cording
Fold-over crimps
Clasp

Tools
Flat-nose pliers
Wire cutters
Scissors
Twist 'n' Curl™

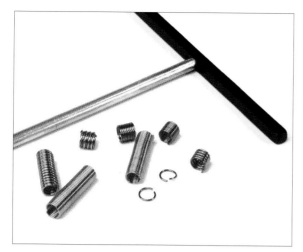

1 Using the largest mandrel on the Twist 'n' Curl™, make two 1½-inch peach coils, two ³/₈-inch fuchsia coils, one 1-inch two-color coil, two ¼-inch two-color coils, and two fuschia jump rings.

2 Cut the velvet cording to neck size plus ½ inch for ease. Use pliers to secure a fold-over crimp on each end of the cording.

3 Thread all of the coils onto the cording as shown, spacing the coils approximately ½- to ³/₄-inch apart and 3 inches from each end.

4 With pliers, attach jump rings and clasps to the crimps on each end of the necklace.

ALTERNATE COIL CHOKER

WHAT YOU'LL NEED

Wire

Colored copper wire
20-gauge Burgundy
20-gauge Gun Metal
24-gauge Black

Brass wire
20-gauge Non-Tarnishing
   Brass

Materials
18-inches of ⅛-inch
   leather lace
Hook-and-eye clasp

Beads
Twelve ⅜-inch cylinder
   beads, gun metal

Tools
Round- and flat-nose pliers
Wire cutters
Scissors
Wire Worker™

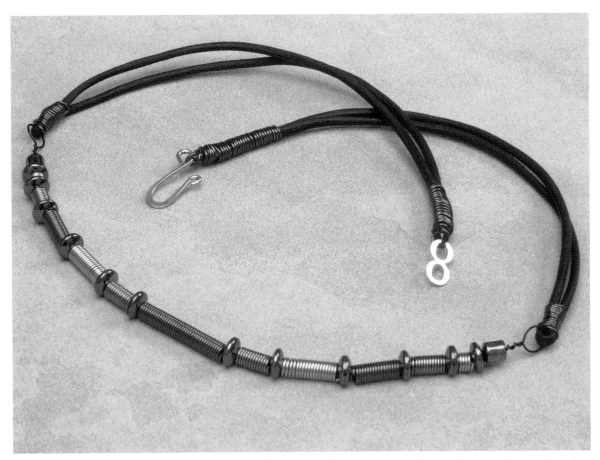

Using the smallest mandrel on the Wire Worker™, make two ½-inch and one 1-inch burgundy coils, make two ½-inch and two ¼-inch brass coils, and make four ⅜-inch gun metal coils. Thread all of the coils and beads onto the 24-gauge wire as shown. Cut the wire and loop the ends. Cut two 9-inch leather laces. Fold each lace in half, then thread a 24-gauge wire loop onto the middle. Secure the folded lace by wire-wrapping the ends. Use the wire tails to attach a hook-and-eye clasp.

Teardrop Necklace

This pretty beaded
necklace has a rather
feminine look. Its
delicate wire flower
design has a classic
and timeless appeal.

SKILL LEVEL
Challenging

WHAT YOU'LL NEED

Wire

Brass wire
20-gauge Non-Tarnishing
Brass
22-gauge Non-Tarnishing
Brass

Materials
Hook-and-eye clasp

Beads
Three $^3/_8$-inch teardrop
beads, amethyst
Forty-one $^1/_8$- to $^1/_{16}$-inch
round glass beads, clear
Twenty-one $^1/_8$- to
$^1/_{16}$-inch round glass
beads, amethyst

Tools
Round- and flat-nose
pliers
Wire cutters
Olympus WigJig™
Olympus WigJig™ peg
pattern
Twist 'n' Curl™

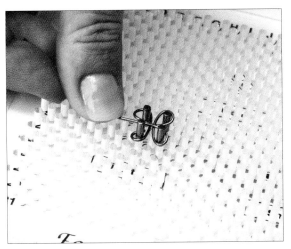

1 Position the jig over the pattern and use 20-gauge wire to make eighteen ¹/₂-inch 4-peg jig flower designs (micro) and one ³/₄-inch 4-peg jig flower (small) design. Cut the excess wire.

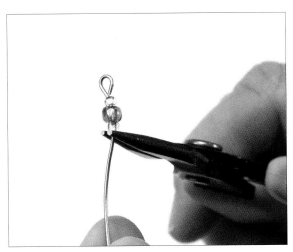

2 Using 22-gauge wire, make nineteen eyepins with two clear and one amethyst bead. Use round pliers to loop the wire ends. Make one eyepin with two amethyst and two clear beads, and one eyepin with one clear bead.

3 Make a hook-and-eye clasp using 2¹/₂-inch lengths of 20-gauge wire (see page 26).

4 Using the medium-size mandrel on the Twist 'n' Curl™ and 20-gauge wire, make three jump rings. Connect the jump rings to the teardrop beads, then connect one teardrop-ring to a three-bead eyepin. Connect the teardrop rings to the largest jig design as shown.

5 Connect all of the components to make one long chain, alternating the jig designs and the bead pins and centering the four-bead pin.

6 Attach the one-bead pin to the top of the teardrop component, then secure the component to the center of the four-bead pin. Connect the hook-and-eye clasp to the necklace ends.

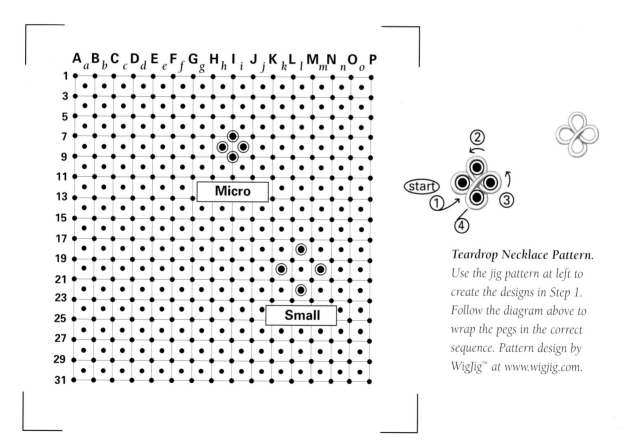

Teardrop Necklace Pattern. Use the jig pattern at left to create the designs in Step 1. Follow the diagram above to wrap the pegs in the correct sequence. Pattern design by WigJig™ at www.wigjig.com.

Rainbow Choker

Using wires in a rainbow of colors, you can create a great-looking choker. Vary the colors to suit your mood and wardrobe.

SKILL LEVEL
Intermediate

WHAT YOU'LL NEED

Wire

Colored silver wire
20-gauge Peach
20-gauge Orchid
20-gauge Blue
20-gauge Seafoam Green
22-gauge Peacock Blue

Brass wire
20-gauge Non-Tarnishing Brass

Materials
18-inches of $1/8$-inch leather lace
Fold-over crimps

Tools
Round- and flat-nose pliers
Wire cutters
Scissors
Wire Worker™

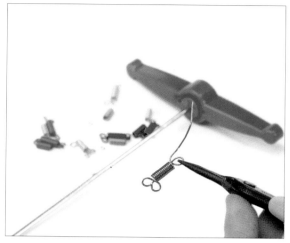

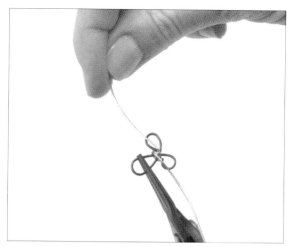

1 Using the smallest mandrel on the Wire Worker™, make three ¹/₂-inch coils each in blue, orchid, and green, and four ¹/₂-inch peach coils. Cut a 2¹/₂-inch wire for each coil. Insert the same color of wire into each coil and double loop each end. Cut off excess wire if necessary. Separate the loops.

2 Using the orchid wire, make two oblong clasps (see page 27). Secure the clasps with peach wire. Make 24 green jump rings using smallest mandrel on the Wire Worker™.

3 Use the jump rings to connect the loops at the top and bottom of the coils, alternating the colors of the coils.

4 Cut two 9-inch leather laces. Fold each lace in half, then thread an oblong clasp onto the middle. Secure the lace at the fold by wrapping with 22-gauge blue wire. Cut off the excess wire. Attach crimps with flat-nose pliers to the doubled ends of the laces. Make a hook-and-eye clasp from brass wire (see page 26), and attach to the crimps.

Eyeglass Chain

This colorful eyeglass chain will perfectly complement any style of glasses. Make a chain to brighten and refurbish some old standbys or to add whimsy to your summer shades.

SKILL LEVEL
Beginner

WHAT YOU'LL NEED

Wire

Colored silver wire
18-gauge Peacock Blue
18-gauge Fuchsia
18-gauge Tangerine
18-gauge Lemon
18-gauge Seafoam Green

Materials
Eyeglass holders

Tools
Round- and flat-nose pliers
Wire cutters
Twist 'n' Curl™

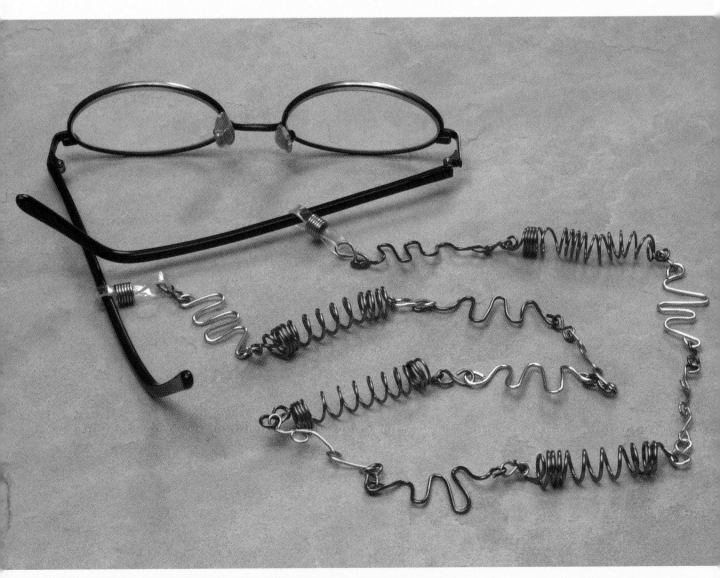

1 *Using the largest mandrel on the Twist 'n' Curl™, make two 1-inch coils each in blue and fuchsia. Stretch the coils slightly and loop the ends.*

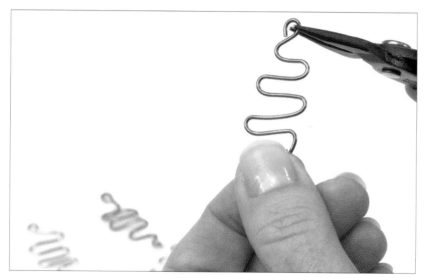

2 *Using pliers, make three 1-inch wiggles each in tangerine and lemon. Loop the wire ends.*

3 *Make fourteen ³/8-inch S-hooks in all colors of wire (see page 29).*

4 *Using round-nose pliers, make three looped shapes from 1³/₄-inch lengths of green wire.*

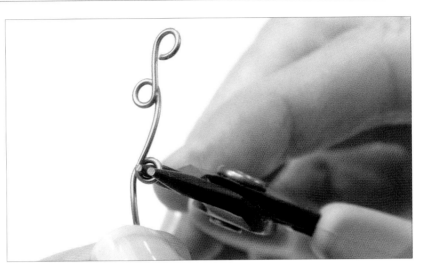

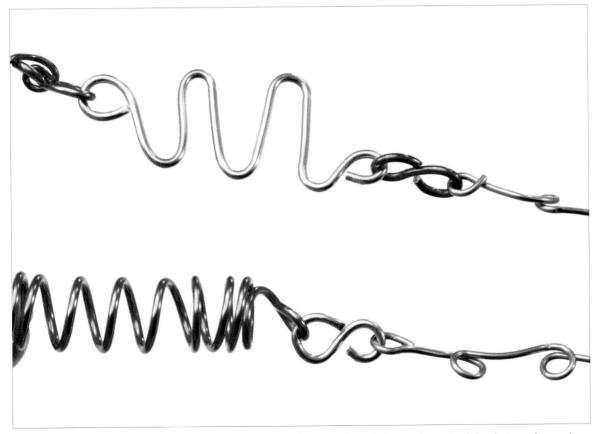

5 *Connect all of the components with S-hooks, alternating shapes as desired. Secure the ends of the chain to the eyeglass holders and attach to glasses.*

Beads and Bows Chain

The stunning beads and bows motif of this necklace is simply formed by shaping coiled wire into a figure-eight design. If desired, vary the look by adding larger beads or more colors of wire.

SKILL LEVEL
Challenging

WHAT YOU'LL NEED

Wire

Colored silver wire
24-gauge Peacock Blue
24-gauge Seafoam Green
20-gauge Seafoam Green

Beads

One dichroic stained glass
   bead, blues/greens
Eighty-nine seed beads,
   blue and aqua
Eleven $1/4$-inch tube
   beads, blue and aqua

Tools

Round- and flat-nose pliers
Wire cutters
Large embroidery needle

1 Using the needle and 24-gauge wires, make twenty ¹/₂-inch coils each in blue and green.

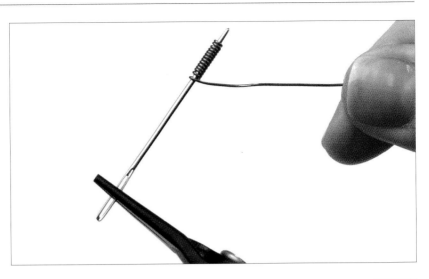

2 Thread a green coil, three seed beads, then a blue coil onto 24-gauge wire. Loop and secure the wire end. Cut the wire from the spool, leaving a 2-inch tail.

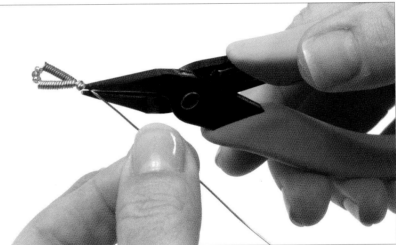

3 Thread a blue seed bead, a green coil, three seed beads, and a blue coil onto the 24-gauge wire tail. Loop the wire and secure it at the base of the first loop to create a bow. Cut off any excess wire.

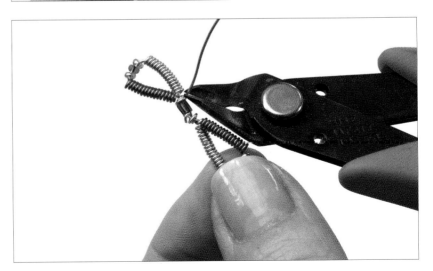

4 Using 20-gauge wire, make eleven eyepins with two seeds and one tube bead. Connect the bows with the beaded pins to make the necklace chain.

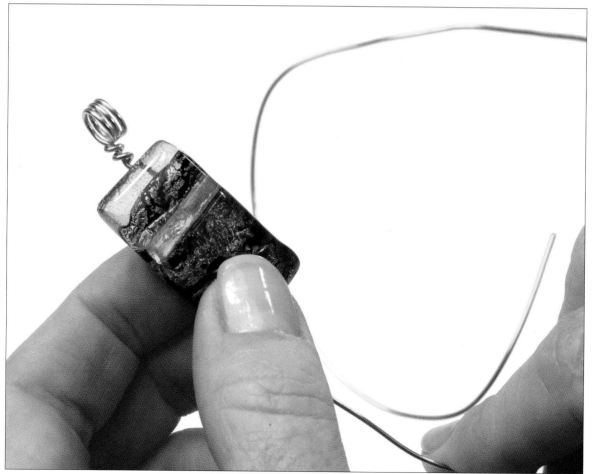

5 Cut a 20-inch length of 20-gauge wire and make a bail at one end (see page 26). Position the bail behind the dichroic bead and wire-wrap the bead. Secure the bead and cut off the excess wire. Hang the wire-wrapped bead from the chain.

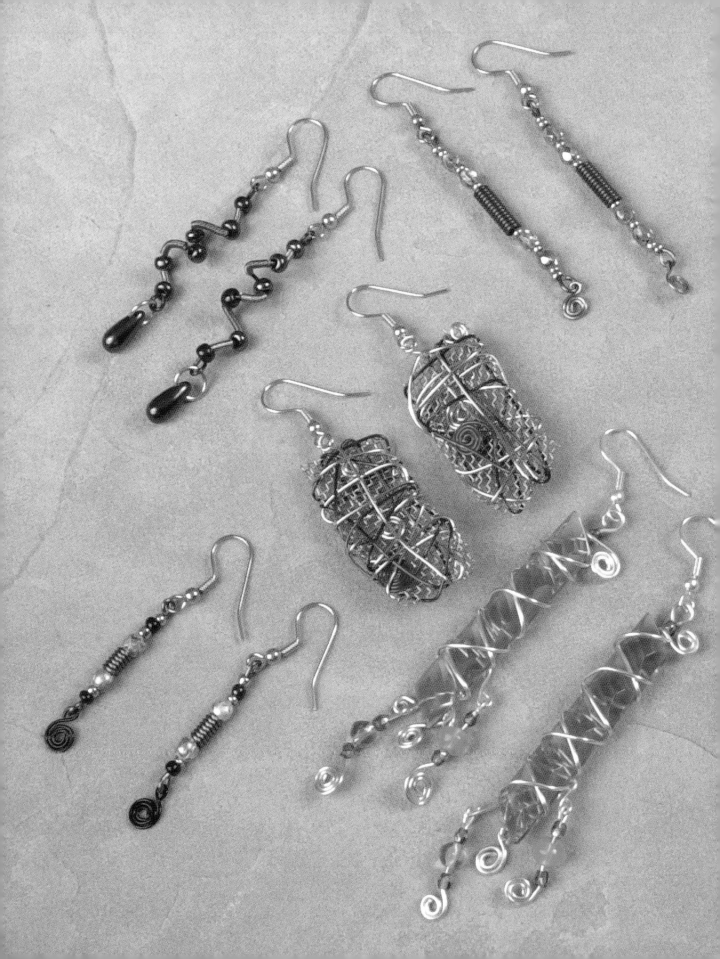

Earrings

Vintage Glass Earrings

Search bead shops, flea markets, and estate sales for unique elements to enhance your jewelry. These dazzling earrings were made from antique pieces of glass that I collected over the years.

SKILL LEVEL
Intermediate

WHAT YOU'LL NEED

Wire

Silver wire
20-gauge Non-Tarnishing Silver

Materials
French hook ear wires

Tools
Round- and flat-nose pliers
Wire cutters

Beads
Two 2-inch pieces antique beveled glass
Four ³/₈-inch round glass beads, blue
Ten ¹/₈-inch glass beads, iridescent

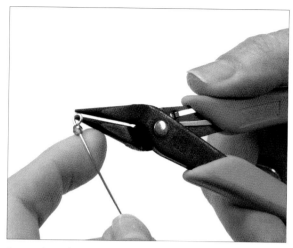

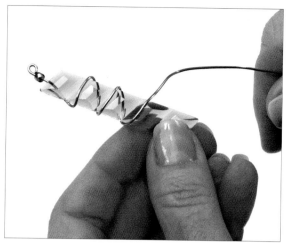

1 Working from the spool, thread a small bead onto the wire and loop the end with round-nose pliers.

2 Move the bead against the loop, then begin wrapping the wire around a piece of beveled glass. Start by working down the glass, then cross the wire over itself and work up the glass.

3 Cut the wire, leaving a 1-inch tail. Loop the end of the tail with round-nose pliers and spiral the wire. With flat-nose pliers, twist the spiral around the top wire wrap to secure it in place.

4 Make two wire and bead spirals and one looped spiral and attach them to the bottom wire wrap so they dangle. Attach an ear wire to the top loop. Repeat the steps to make the second earring.

Coil Cylinder Earrings

These lightweight earrings are fast and fun to make and can be color coordinated to match any outfit.

SKILL LEVEL
Beginner

WHAT YOU'LL NEED

Wire

Colored copper wire
22-gauge Burgundy
20-gauge Gun Metal

Brass wire
22-gauge Non-Tarnishing Brass

Materials
French hook ear wires

Tools
Round-nose pliers
Wire cutters
Wire Worker™

Beads
Eight $3/8$-inch round glass beads, iridescent
Fourteen seed beads, gold

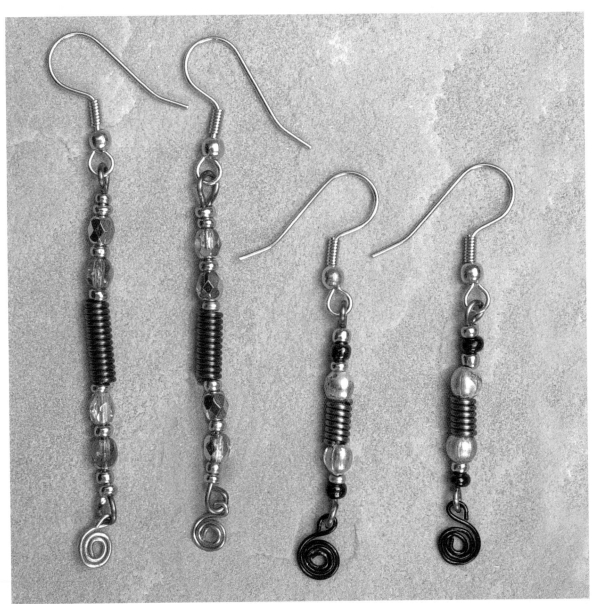

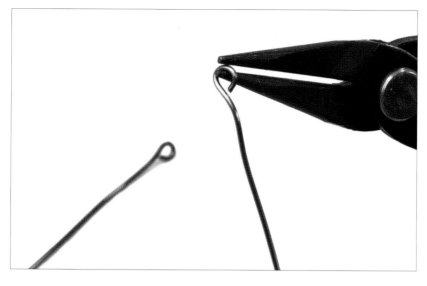

1   Cut two 2¹/₂-inch lengths of 20-gauge wire. Use round-nose pliers to form wire into eyepins.

2   Using Wire Worker™, make two ¹/₂-inch burgundy coils. Make two ¹/₄-inch brass spirals and loop the ends with round-nose pliers.

3   Using the photograph as your guide, thread beads and a coil onto each eyepin and loop the ends of the pins. Attach an ear hook on the top of each earring and a spiral on the bottom.

Funky Teardrop Earrings

Fun and whimsical best describes these beaded wire earrings. They are very simple to make and look great with almost every outfit.

SKILL LEVEL
Intermediate

WHAT YOU'LL NEED

Wire

Colored silver wire
28-gauge Peacock Blue
28-gauge Plum
20-gauge Orchid
20-gauge Seafoam Green

Materials
French hook ear wires

Tools
Round- and flat-nose
   pliers
Wire cutters
Small sewing needle
Twist 'n' Curl™

Beads
Twelve ¼-inch round
   glass beads, iridescent
Two ¾-inch teardrop
   beads, iridescent

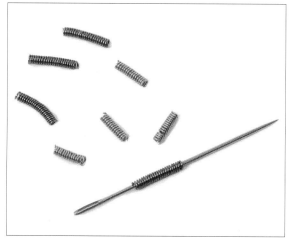

1   Wrap the 28-gauge wires around the needle to make six ¼-inch blue and four ½-inch plum coils.

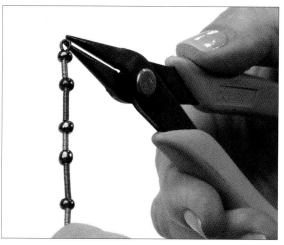

2   Thread six round beads and five coils, alternating beads and coils, onto the 20-gauge orchid wire. Cut the wire and loop the ends. Repeat step to make the second earring.

3   Using the smallest mandrel of the Twist 'n' Curl™, wrap the beaded wires around the mandrel to create loose, irregular coils.

4   Make two green jump rings using the smallest mandrel on the Twist 'n' Curl™ and attach them to the teardrop beads. Attach a beaded jump ring to the bottom of each earring and an ear hook to the top.

Wire Mesh Earrings

Wire mesh comes in several colors and gauges, allowing for endless design applications. Experiment with different combinations of wire and mesh to create a variety of one-of-a-kind jewelry pieces.

SKILL LEVEL
Beginner

WHAT YOU'LL NEED

Materials

Colored silver wire
22-gauge Peach
28-gauge Fuchsia

Materials
French hook ear wires
Decorative metal mesh,
    classic brass

Tools
Round- and flat-nose pliers
Wire cutters
Scissors
Twist 'n' Curl™

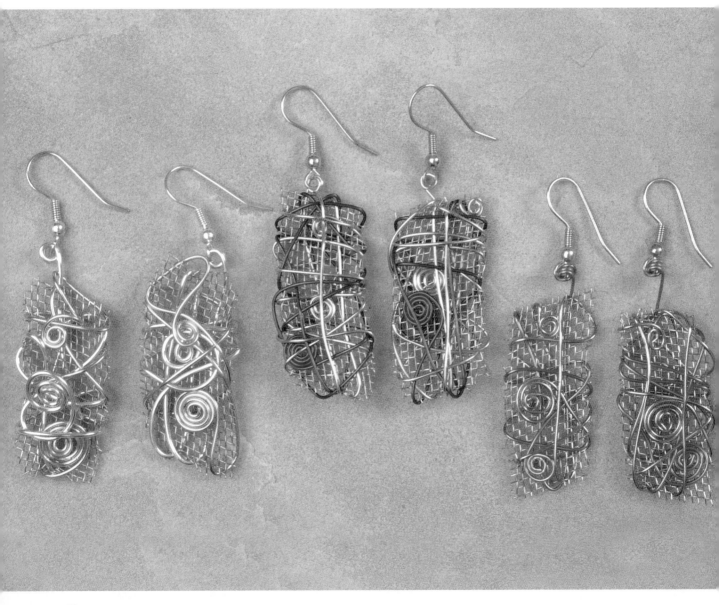

1 With scissors, cut the wire mesh into a 1½-inch by ¾-inch rectangle.

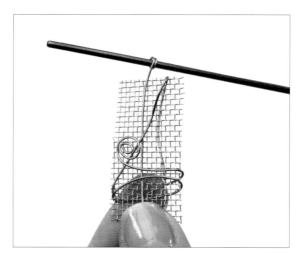

2 Loop and spiral the end of the fuchsia wire. Press the spiral onto the mesh and wrap the wire in different directions. When the mesh is secure, hold the wire at the top of the mesh, loop it around the smallest mandrel of the Twist 'n' Curl™ two times, then cut the wire at the base of the loop.

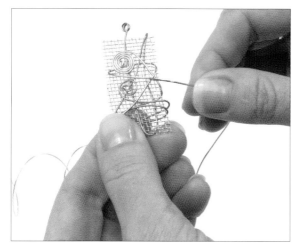

3 Repeat step 2 using peach wire and omitting the loop. When the mesh is secure, cut, loop, and spiral the wire, then press it to the mesh.

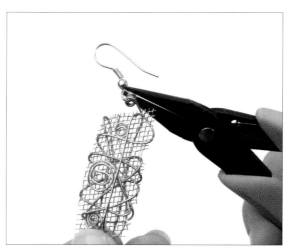

4 Attach an ear hook to the top loop. Repeat the steps to make a second earring.

Wire-Wrapped Bead Rings

These pretty silver bead rings are surprisingly simple to make. With only a few quick wraps, you can create a lovely piece of jewelry.

SKILL LEVEL
Intermediate

WHAT YOU'LL NEED

Wire

Silver wire
18-gauge Non-Tarnishing Silver

Materials
Beacon's Gem-Tac Glue™

Beads
One 1/4-inch round glass beads, blue

Tools
Round- and flat-nose pliers
Wire cutters
Dowel (ring size in diameter)
Metal file

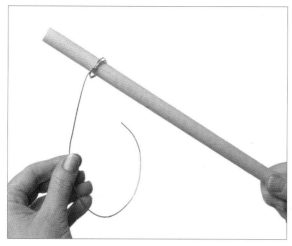

1 *Working from the spool, double wrap the wire around the dowel and cut the wire, leaving a 7-inch tail. Secure the short end of the wire at the base of the ring.*

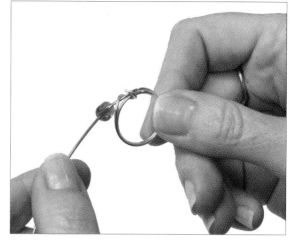

2 *Thread a bead onto the long tail and position the bead at the top of the ring. Wrap the long tail onto wire at the base of the bead to secure.*

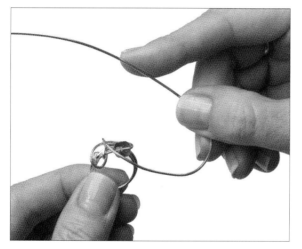

3 *Randomly weave the long tail into loops in and around the bead. Cut off the excess wire and tuck in the tail. File the wire ends as needed.*

For an alternate style, follow the steps above, but instead of looping the wire in step 3, spiral the wire in one direction to a desired diameter. If a bead will not fit the wire, spiral the wire around itself, then glue a bead onto center of the spiral. Cut off the excess wire and tuck in the tail. File the wire ends as needed.

Double-Wrapped Bead Ring

What can be more special than making your
own friendship ring? It is the kind of gift loved
ones will cherish forever.

SKILL LEVEL
Intermediate

WHAT YOU'LL NEED

Wire

Silver wire
18-gauge Non-Tarnishing
    Silver

Beads
One ¹/₄-inch round glass
    bead, green

Tools
Flat-nose pliers
Wire cutters
Dowel (ring size in
    diameter)
Metal file

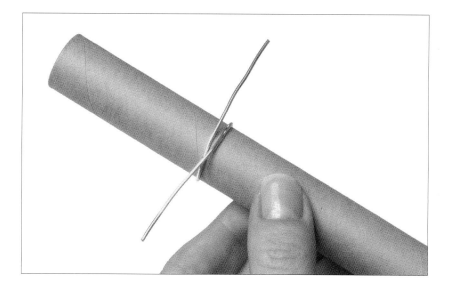

1 Working from the spool, wrap the wire once around the dowel. Cut the wire, leaving two 1¹/₂-inch tails beyond the diameter of the dowel.

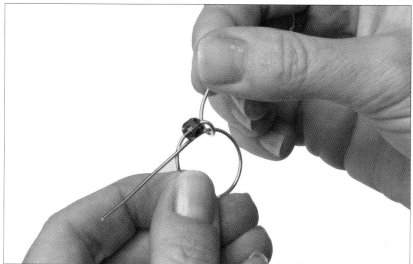

2 Thread the bead onto the wire and position the bead at the top of the ring. Wrap one tail around the wire at the base of the bead to secure it in place.

3 Using pliers, wrap the opposite tail under the bead and around the wire at the base of the bead. Cut off the excess wire and tuck in the tail. File the wire ends as needed.

Simple Ring

The creative use of smaller beads and two colors
of wire can create a delicate and elegant ring.

SKILL LEVEL
Beginner

WHAT YOU'LL NEED

Wire

Silver wire
18-gauge Non-Tarnishing
  Silver
28-gauge Gold

Beads
Twelve seed beads, blue

Tools
Flat-nose pliers
Wire cutters
Dowel (ring size in
  diameter)
Metal file

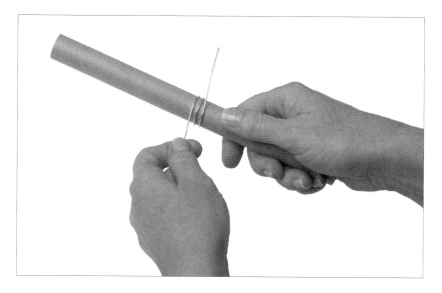

1 Working from the spool, wrap the 18-gauge wire three times around the dowel. Cut the wire, leaving two 1¹/₂-inch tails beyond the diameter of the dowel.

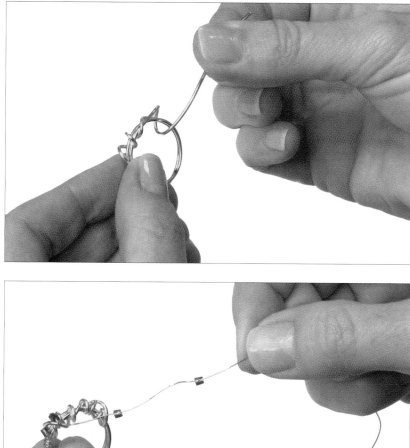

2 Wrap the ends of the wire over and under the top of the ring. Cut off the excess wire and tuck in the tails. File the wire ends as needed.

3 Thread the beads onto the 28-gauge wire. Secure the wire end to the ring with pliers and wrap the beaded wire over and under the top of the ring. Secure the end with pliers and cut the excess wire. File the wire ends as needed.

Hair Accessories

Wire-Wrapped Hair Sticks

These wonderful hair sticks were inspired by the sugar sticks you use to sweeten coffee. Make an assortment of fun and colorful sticks to dress up buns and other hair styles.

SKILL LEVEL
Beginner

WHAT YOU'LL NEED

Wire

Colored silver wire
22-gauge Orchid
28-gauge Plum

Materials
Hair Sticks
Beacon's Gem-Tac Glue™

Beads
100 seed beads, green

Tools
Wire cutters

1 Working off the spool, thread a minimum of 10 inches' worth of seed beads onto the 28-gauge wire. Secure the end of the beaded wire on the top of the stick and wrap the wire firmly around the stick, keeping the beads together. Cut the wire, leaving a ½-inch tail. Tuck in the tail.

2 Wrap the 22-gauge wire around the beads to create an orb-shaped cage, allowing the beads to show through. Wrap the wire tightly at the base of the orb to secure it in place. Cut off the excess wire and tuck in the tail.

3 For added reinforcement, slip the wire orb off the stick and apply glue to the top of the stick. Reattach the orb and allow the glue to set.

Wire and Bead Hair Comb

Hair combs enhanced with wire and beads make classic and stylish hair accessories. Experiment with different wire and bead combinations to find the perfect complement to your hair color.

SKILL LEVEL
Intermediate

WHAT YOU'LL NEED

Wire

Colored silver wire
28-gauge Gold

Materials
Hair comb

Beads
250 seed beads, green
Fifteen to eighteen
   1/8-inch glass beads,
   burgundy

Tools
Wire cutters

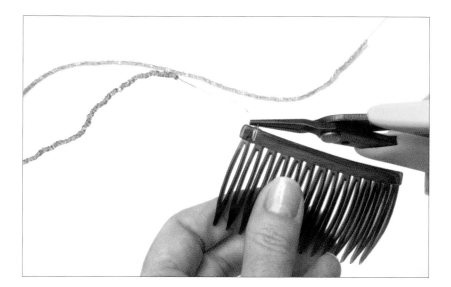

1 *Working off the spool, thread at least 20 inches' worth of seed beads onto the wire. Secure the end of the wire onto the comb. Begin wrapping the wire loosely around the head of the comb to create an airy effect.*

2 *Slide beads up the wire with every other wrap and continue to wrap loosely. Wrap the entire comb, then cut off the excess wire, leaving a ½-inch tail. Tuck in the tail.*

3 *Thread about 15 or 18 glass beads onto the wire and repeat steps 1 and 2, wrapping the beaded wire over and around the seed beads.*

Tubular Hair Barrette

Simple wire coils can turn a barrette into an interesting and attractive hair ornament. Vary the look by using one or several colors of wire.

SKILL LEVEL
Beginner

WHAT YOU'LL NEED

Wire

Colored silver wire
20-gauge Seafoam Green
20-gauge Peach
20-gauge Non-Tarnishing
  Silver
28-gauge Seafoam Green

Materials
One 2½-inch metal
  barrette back

Tools
Wire cutters
Twist 'n' Curl™

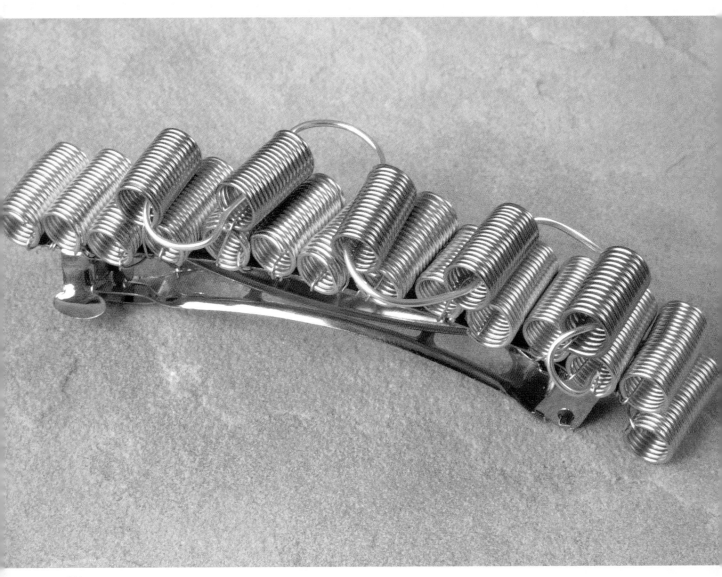

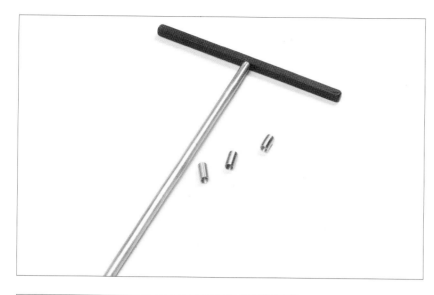

1 Using the largest mandrel on the Twist 'n' Curl™, make fourteen ³/₄-inch green coils and five ³/₄-inch peach coils.

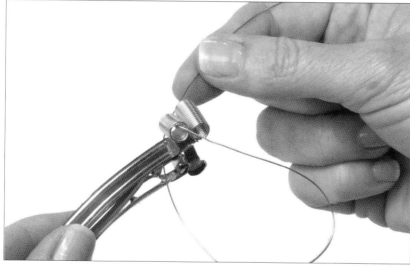

2 Thread 28-gauge wire through the green coils and secure the coils to the barrette by positioning the coils on top one at a time and wrapping the wire over and under the hair barrette.

3 Cut a 7-inch length of 20-gauge silver wire and secure one end to the third green coil. Thread one peach coil onto the wire and bend the wire at the edge of the coil. Continue adding coils one at a time and bending the wire between the coils. Thread wire through the last coil and secure the wire to the twelfth green coil.

Whimsical Hair Barrettes

What little girl can resist such cool and crafty hair barrettes? Follow the same technique to make large and small barrettes in an assortment of bright colors.

SKILL LEVEL
Beginner

WHAT YOU'LL NEED

Wire

Colored silver wire
28-gauge Aqua
28-gauge Rose
28-gauge Blue

Materials
One 2¹/₂-inch metal barrette back
Double-face super-sticky tape
Small bowl

Beads
One package Teenie Weenie Beadies™ "No Hole" glass beads

Tools
Wire cutters
¹/₂-inch diameter dowel (or size according to barrette)
Scissors

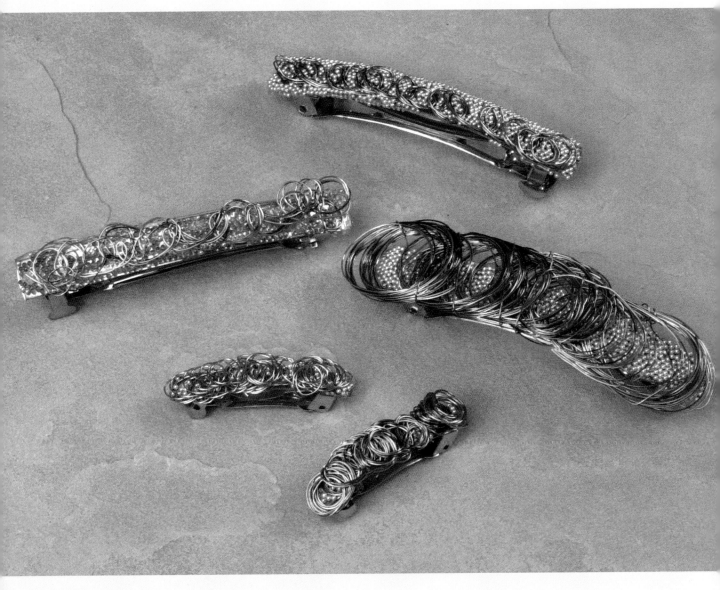

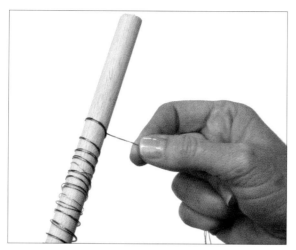

1 *Using all three colors of wire, wrap the wires around the dowel approximately 20 to 25 times.*

2 *Remove the wire from the dowel and carefully stretch and flatten the coils to the length of the barrette. Cut off the loose ends of wire.*

3 *Cut a strip of tape to the length of the barrette. Adhere the strip along the top of the barrette and remove the protective backing. Press the barrette into the beads. Continue to press and roll until the entire barrette is covered with beads.*

4 *Cut a 20-inch length of wire. Secure the wire to the top end of the opened barrette. Place the coils over the beads, then wrap the wire around the coils and barrette to secure them in place. Cut off the excess wire and tuck in the tail.*

Flower Hair Clips

Flower power is the theme for these delightful hair clips. Group several colorful clips together to create a whimsical hair bouquet.

SKILL LEVEL
Beginner

WHAT YOU'LL NEED

Wire

Colored silver wire
22-gauge Peach

Colored copper wire
22-gauge Red

Materials
Hair clip
Beacon's Gem-Tac Glue™

Beads
One pronged stud,
    butterfly or other design

Tools
Flat-nose pliers
Wire cutters
Twist 'n' Curl™

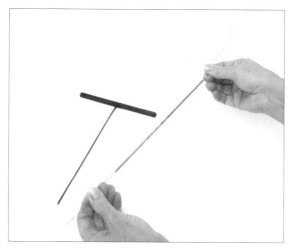

1 Using the red wire and the smallest mandrill of the Twist 'n' Curl™, make one 4-inch coil. Cut the wire, allowing for two 2-inch tails. Stretch the coil slightly to loosen the tension.

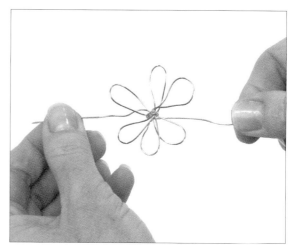

2 Loop the peach wire into one-inch flower petals and wrap the center to secure the petals, allowing for two 2-inch tails.

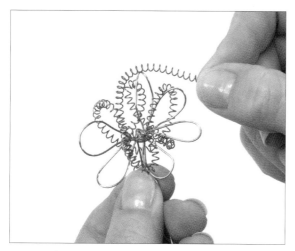

3 Loop the coiled wire around the flower and wrap the wire around the center, using pliers to secure it in place.

4 Attach the stud to the center of the flower. Use pliers to press the prongs closed, grabbing as much wire as possible. Wrap the wire tails around the base of the clip to secure the flower in place. Apply glue for added reinforcement.

Suppliers

Listed at right are the manufacturers of and suppliers for many of the materials used in this book. Most of these companies sell their products exclusively to craft and jewelry supply retailers, which are a consumer's most dependable sources for wire jewelrymaking supplies. Your local retailer can advise you on purchases, and if you need something they don't have in stock they will usually order it for you. If you can't find a store in your area that carries a particular item or will accept a request for an order, or if you need special assistance, a manufacturer will direct you to the retailer nearest you that carries their products and will try to answer any technical questions you might have.

Artistic Wire Ltd.
1210 Harrison Ave.
La Grange Park, Illinois 60526
630/530-7567
Wire, tools

Beacon Adhesives
Orders: Signature Crafts
800/865-7238
Glues

Dichroic Fused Beads
   by Tonya Rilling
Buffalo Stampede
3604 Bent Tree Court
Wilmington, North Carolina
   28405-8800
Beads

Helwig Industries, LLC
P.O. Box 5306
Arlington, Virginia 22205
800/579-WIRE
Tools

The Leather Factory
Tejas Brand Leather Lace
P.O. Box 50429
Ft. Worth, Texas 76105
877/LEATHER
Leather lace

LeFranc & Bourgeois
11 Constitution Avenue
Piscataway, New Jersey
   08855-0941
800/445-4278
Wire mesh

NSI
National Science Industries, Ltd.
910 Orlando Avenue
West Hempstead, New York 11552
516/678-1700
www.bedazzler.com
BeDazzler™ metal studs

Rings & Things
Box 450
Spokane, Washington 99210
800/366-2156
Beads (wholesale only)

Scotti-Crafts
P.O. Box 3550
Mt. Vernon, New York 10553
800/862-8721
Beads

Twist 'n' Curl
800/717-4156
Tools

Xuron Corp
60 Industrial Park Road
Saco, Maine 07072
207/283-1401
Tools

GETTING IN TOUCH
Kathy Peterson
www.kathypeterson.com

Andy Newitt
Film Light & Magic, Inc.
1535 Cypress Drive
Jupiter, Florida 33469
561/748-8574

Index

ABOUT THE AUTHOR

The work of craft designer **Kathy Peterson** has been published in numerous craft and women's magazines and has been featured on several nationally broadcast television shows, including *The Christopher Lowell Show, Home Matters* (both on the Discovery Channel), *Your Home Studio, Aleene's Creative Living* (both on TNN), *The Carol Duvall Show, Today at Home,* and *Decorating with Style* (on HGTV). Kathy is also the "Trends" columnist for *ProCrafter* magazine and the host and producer of her own television show, *Town & Country Crafts with Kathy Peterson* (on GoodLife TV). She lives in Tequesta, Florida.

ABOUT THE PHOTOGRAPHER

Andy Newitt is a commercial still life photographer whose company, Film Light & Magic, Inc., is based in Jupiter, Florida.